# VIII Fighter Command at War *'The Long Reach'*

SERIES EDITOR: TONY HOLMES

OSPREY AIRCRAFT OF THE ACES • 31

# VIII Fighter Command at War 'The Long Reach'

Compiled by Michael O'Leary

OSPREY
AVIATION

**Front cover**
At 1120 hrs on 23 March 1944, P-51B Mustangs from the 4th Fighter Group (FG), led by the redoubtable Col Don Blakeslee, rendezvoused at 24,000 ft with B-17 Flying Fortresses from the 3rd Bomb Division west of Hanover. The 'heavies' were heading for Brunswick, and the fighters had been allocated the role of Target Support. A group of P-38 Lightnings was also in the area tasked with the same mission. As the bombers came into view, Capt Duane 'Bee' Beeson, CO of the 334th Fighter Squadron (FS), spotted 25+ Bf 109s and Fw 190s pressing home their attacks on the beleaguered B-17s. He immediately ordered his squadron to attack, punching off his aircraft's 75-gallon drop tanks and opening the throttle of his P-51B-5 (43-6819). The ensuing fight was intense, and took the fighters down to 3000 ft. The 4th FG came out the clear victors, however, claiming ten German aircraft destroyed without loss. Beeson noted in his logbook, 'I got two '109s and damaged a train. Had a hell of a fight with one of them. Lots of fun!' Sadly, the bombers did not fare so well, for out of the 224 despatched almost all suffered some damage, and 16 were lost
(*Cover artwork by Iain Wyllie*)

For a catalogue of all titles published by Osprey Publishing please contact us at:

**Osprey Direct UK,**
**P.O. Box 140, Wellingborough,**
**Northants NN8 4ZA, UK**
E-mail: info@ospreydirect.co.uk

**Osprey Direct USA,**
**P.O. Box 130, Sterling Heights,**
**MI 48311-0130, USA**
E-mail: info@ospreydirectusa.com

Or visit our website:
**www.ospreypublishing.com**

First published in Great Britain in 2000 by Osprey Publishing
1st Floor, Elms Court, Chapel Way, Botley, Oxford, OX2 9LP
E-mail: info@ospreypublishing.com

ISBN 1 85532 907 7

Edited by Tony Holmes
Page Design by TT Designs, T & B Truscott
Cover Artwork by Iain Wyllie
Aircraft Profiles by Chris Davey, the late Keith Fretwell, Tom Tullis, John Weal and Iain Wyllie
Figure Artwork by Mike Chappell
Scale Drawings by Mark Styling
Photo Captions by Tony Holmes
Plates Commentaries by Jerry Scutts, John Stanaway and Tony Holmes
Origination by Grasmere Digital Imaging, Leeds, UK
Printed through Bookbuilders, Hong Kong

00 01 02 03 04 05   10 9 8 7 6 5 4 3 2 1

ACKNOWLEDGEMENTS
The Editor wishes to particularly thank Sam Sox for the provision of many of the photographs which appear in this volume. Other contributors of note include Dick Martin, Martin Bowman, Roger Freeman, Ian Phillips, Marc Hamel, Bill Hess, Tom Ivie, Garry Fry, Tom Frisque, John Stanaway, George Carpenter and the 20th and 352nd Fighter Group Associations.

EDITOR'S NOTE
The first-hand accounts that form the 'backbone' of this volume were originally compiled by the USAAF in the spring of 1944. In order to keep within the period in which this document was created, only photographs of aircraft and pilots taken up to 30 June 1944 are included. Similarly, the profile artwork featured also depicts P-47s, P-38s and P-51s up to the end of June.

To make this best-selling series as authoritative as possible, the editor would be interested in hearing from any individual who may have relevant photographs, documentation or first-hand experiences relating to aircrews, and their aircraft, of the various theatres of war. Any material used will be credited to its original source. Please write to Tony Holmes at 10 Prospect Road, Sevenoaks, Kent, TN13 3UA, Great Britain, or by e-mail at tony.holmes@osprey-jets.freeserve.co.uk

# CONTENTS

# AUTHOR'S INTRODUCTION

Sometimes history can be found in unusual places. While browsing through a Pasadena, California, flea market, I came across an item that I instantly recognised as a World War 2 US government publication. Thinking it might be a flight manual for a combat aircraft, I quickly grabbed the document. However, thumbing through the yellowing pages I found that I had something much more unusual.

The document, titled *The Long Reach*, was a survey of two-dozen fighter pilots focusing on the tactics that they employed against the Luftwaffe. Needless to say, this was an extremely important volume, for it effectively laid down the ground rules for the tough long-range battle that took place over Germany between Luftwaffe fighters and American Thunderbolts, Lightnings and Mustangs.

Quickly purchasing the manual, I began reading it that night. I was both fascinated by the amount of information it contained and inspired by the individual initiative undertaken by the American combat airman. After discussing the manual with Osprey's Aviation Editor, Tony Holmes, a decision was made to publish the document with just standard editing (the original I had purchased was full of hand-written notes and additions – I wonder who the pilot was?). No illustrations were featured in *The Long Reach*, so most of the wonderful photographs contained within this book are the result of the hard work of George Carpenter, Dick Martin, Sam Sox and Marc Hamel. All four individuals have been compiling rare wartime photographs for years, and Sam's magical work in the dark room has made even the most faded of photos snap back into full life.

This book is dedicated to the American fighter pilot – to those who made it back home to base and to those who didn't.

Michael O'Leary
Los Angeles, California
September 2000

# PERIOD PREFACE

## Major General W E KEPNER
## VIII Fighter Command

The daylight onslaught by steadily increasing fleets of American heavy bombers and long-range fighters upon vital targets deep in enemy territory, and the concentrated fury of the Luftwaffe's stepped-up fighter forces in their effort to prevent it, made inevitable the greatest head-on clash of air forces in history. The long, desperate battle which resulted is not yet over, but it is now clear that the courage and the destructive 0.50s of our bomber crews and the skill, daring, and teamwork of our long-range escort fighter pilots are driving the enemy to the ground. The tactics of these fighter pilots, unique because of their unprecedented mission, are the subject of this publication, and some 24 of the most outstanding of them, either by their own writing or their guidance, are its authors.

Without going into the development of the VIII Fighter Command in England from its first few groups to its present ability to escort a single mission with a thousand fighters, it is nonetheless necessary to pin the comments herein down to the particular phase of the European air war to which they apply. The fighter pilots quoted are taking for granted some knowledge of the new requirements, equipment and techniques which have kept pace with the rapid expansion of the opposing forces and the mounting ferocity of the battle.

The initial stage of fighter escort in this theatre presented nothing new in the basic escort principle as established by the RAF and by our own forces in other theatres. It did represent the many unique and

Maj Gen William Kepner assumed command of VIII Fighter Command from Brig Gen Frank O'D Hunter on 29 August 1943. He was committed to escorting bombers all the way to Berlin and back from the moment he took charge (*352nd FG Association*)

original ideas contributed by all as to the implementation of the old fundamental principles – particularly in finding a wary enemy, then developing teamwork by all the units and individuals comprising any unit down to a single 'pair'.

During this stage, our P-47 Thunderbolts provided protection for the bombers on short penetrations of some 165 miles – roughly to Brussels, Cambrai, Paris, Argenton, etc. – and part-way protection to this limit of range as the bombers went out, and again as they came home. The enemy for the most part simply waited to intercept until fuel limitation forced the Thunderbolts to leave, and it was good fortune that the enemy's technique at that time was not well enough developed to stop the bomber fleets, even though the major portion of their journey was unescorted. Of course, valuable experience was gained by our fighter pilots during this period, and certain signal victories gave promise of the fine performance of the P-47 fighter plane and the skill of our pilots, which was to be demonstrated in the months immediately following.

About the 1st of August of last year (1943), two experiments began, one necessitated by the other, which, by some vision and much trial and error, were to make possible the first really long-range fighter escort. These were the use of belly tanks or wing tanks, and the group-by-group relay system.

Putting belly tanks on the Thunderbolts for longer range seems simple enough, but the programme was complicated by tactical considerations. Since our fighters were liable to attack, or be attacked, the minute they crossed the enemy coast, there was hope only of saving the distance out across the Channel, and a tank of but 75 gallons capacity was used for this purpose. The hopes of high Air Force Command were of course looking far beyond this modest achievement, and these hopes received new impetus one day when the 4th Group took a chance and carried their tanks inland, holding them to the moment of combat. 56th and other groups followed suit. With this possibility demonstrated, larger and larger tanks were requested and became available.

Farther and farther went the Thunderbolts along with the Fortresses and Liberators, escorting them 450 miles now to any point within an arc range running approximately through Kiel, Hanover, Karlsruhe, Stuttgart, Vichy, Limoges and La Rochelle. The enemy tried early attacks upon our fighters to force them to drop tanks. It was too costly for him. He relapsed into his policy of avoiding fighter combat whenever possible in order to get at bombers when, in the last reaches of their penetration, they were still unescorted. His opportunity to do this

The use of external fuel tanks greatly increased the effective bomber escort range for VIII Fighter Command P-47s. The 'bathtub' ferrying tank – seen here fitted to a 335th FS/4th FG Thunderbolt – was the first type of external fuel source employed in the ETO. Proving prone to leakage and sometimes failing to release in flight, the 'bathtub' tank (nicknamed the 'baby' by pilots) was only used for a handful of missions in August 1943 (*via Dick Martin*)

352nd FG CO, Col Joe 'Big Red' Mason, greets Brig Gen Kepner upon his arrival at the group's Bodney base in July 1944. Mason led the 'Blue-nosed Bastards of Bodney' from May 1943 until the end of July 1944, claiming exactly five kills in combat. He was awarded the Distinguished Service Cross by visiting US Secretary of War, Henry L Stimson, just prior to leaving the 352nd (*via Marc Hamel*)

Destined for the ETO, much needed P-47Ds move along the final assembly line at Republic's massive Farmingdale plant in New York. The production line was in the process of switching from camouflaged to natural metal aircraft when this photograph was taken in April 1944, hence the stack of unpainted fuselages standing on end in the background. With three production facilities at their disposal, Republic churned out more than 13,000 Thunderbolts in just 45 months (*via Michael O'Leary*)

was now cut down to a very much shorter period on the deepest missions, and on the middle distance missions did not exist at all. Long range escort was actually in being.

Since the faster speed of our fighters caused them to use up their range in a much shorter period of time than bombers covering the same distance, it became necessary to divide up our fighter escort into relays. A group would fly directly to a rendezvous point along the bomber route, stay with the bombers until relieved by another group

An unidentified *Bogue* class escort carrier heads for Liverpool with its precious cargo of P-38Gs and P-47Ds in late 1943. The US Navy's vast fleet of 'Jeep' carriers proved crucial for the rapid transportation of fighters across the Atlantic to the ETO (*both photos via M O'Leary*)

Deck-eye view of another anonymous 'Jeep' carrier. When configured for operating in the escort carrier role, these vessels embarked a mixed air wing of 21+ aircraft, but when transporting USAAF fighters, around 40 could be crowded onto the flightdeck. The outer wing sections for these P-38s would be stored in the hangar bay

or as long as possible, then return more or less directly to base. The long line of bombers was protected not only by the fighter groups assigned for its protection for certain divisions for given periods, but also by the constant stream of fighters en route to rendezvous or returning from escort pretty much along the same route. Experience taught many lessons, and this relay system became a large and permanent feature in the new aerial warfare science of long range escort.

The addition to our fighter force operations in October and December 1943 of two groups of P-38 Lightnings created a new phase. With new built-in fuel capacity adding to their normal long range, the P-38s could go to the bombers' target and provide protection there during the most crucial moments of bombing. Still, there were gaps in the escort. There were not enough P-38s to cover the bombers from the point where the Thunderbolts had finally to leave them and return and still cover the target area, too. Some operational difficulties experienced by the Lightnings flying at high altitudes in the winter season in this theatre added to the limitations, this handicap being overcome to some extent by a fine display of skill and courage by the P-38 pilots and leaders.

Complete long-range fighter escort – round trip from England to Berlin, Munich, and points east – became possible with the addition to the operations of this Command in March 1944 of a number of groups of P-51 Mustangs, by large measure longer in range than any other fighter on the battle fronts, and superior in many other combat characteristics. The circle was now complete. Where the bombers go to bomb, the fighters go to protect them. Together, they wrought, and are wreaking, a vast destruction upon the enemy, and together they have fought him out of the air to the point at least where he dares contest our passage only sporadically, and at moments especially opportune for him.

This outline of the technical phases of long-range fighter escort is not to lose sight of the fact that it has meant determined, courageous, and skilful battle all the way – the greatest offensive fighter battle ever fought, in fact.

The work of the P-38 Lightnings has already been mentioned. The brilliant, devastating accomplishments of the P-51 Mustang are our present enthusiasm. It is perhaps the moment to point out the following fact – by far the larger proportion of our escort fighters to date have been P-47 Thunderbolts, and their share of the 2321 enemy planes destroyed by this Command in combat, with 1496 probably destroyed and damaged, is in ratio to their numbers. If it can be said that the P-38s struck the Luftwaffe in its vitals and the P-51s are giving it the *coup de grace*, it was the Thunderbolt that broke its back. All types are working together under comprehensive plans by the VIII Fighter Command, together with active control by the Wings, and have cornered the German air force to the point where it has to fight.

The comments quoted in this publication were written during the most recent stages of the long-range fighter war as outlined above, and the publication date on the cover (Editor's Note: 29 May 1944) is important to note. Experience and opinion are accurate and authentic as of now. New fighter groups, groups about to become operational, fighter pilots in training and future students of tactics are warned, however, of the rapidly changing techniques, and they must keep

By the spring of 1944 North American Aviation's war-winning Merlin-engined Mustang was arriving in the ETO in great numbers. These cocooned examples were photographed at Bristol's Filton airport on 18 April 1944, the fighters being assembled, test flown and assigned to combat units from this site. Those P-51Bs parked closer to the hangar have been stripped of their anti-corrosion covering to reveal their natural metal finish. Squeezed in amongst the fighters are several Douglas A-20 Havocs that had also been shipped to the UK (*via Michael O'Leary*)

The first 108-US gal Bowater paper composition drop tanks to reach the Mustang-equipped 4th FG wait to be unloaded from a convoy of GMC 'deuce-and-half' trucks at Debden in late May 1944 (*via Dick Martin*)

themselves abreast of them if they wish to have the best and most recent information available. This Command will do whatever is possible and practical by amendment, revision or re-publication to keep up to date.

It should also be pointed out and underlined that this material, although it may aid in creating one, is not a manual of fighter tactics. It is a record of experience from the battle, in passing, of extreme value we believe to every fighter pilot and every fighter leader who will sit in a cockpit in any war theatre in the world. Many differences of opinion will be apparent. Be sure they are real differences, not just differences in expressing a similar idea. There are many comments, for example, as to how to avoid over-shooting. Yet, Capt Beeson says, 'Over-shooting is a very good thing'. But he means, and explains, that speed of attack is a very good thing, and he is seconded in this opinion by Maj Mahurin, Col Zemke, Lt Col Schilling and other great fighters. In general, fighter doctrine is confirmed, and any basic principles are repeated so often that their soundness cannot be doubted.

A fighter pilot may well read these pages with a red pencil in his hand marking a passage here and there with the thought, 'That's for me', then practice, try out and develop the technique until it becomes part of his own, or if it doesn't work out, discard it. It is by such basic learning, plus imagination, experiment and test in combat that all techniques have been developed, and all great fighter pilots have won their many battles.

W E KEPNER, Major General, Commanding
VIII Fighter Command
May 1944

Damp underfoot and misty overhead – these were the conditions that greeted the first Mustang group to arrive in the ETO, the 354th FG. Although assigned to the tactical Ninth Air Force, senior officers (including Maj Gen Kepner) within VIII Fighter Command succeeded in convincing USAAF planners in Washington DC to allow the 'Pioneer Mustang Group' to fly bomber escort missions with the Eighth Air Force. Undertaking its first such mission from Boxted on 5 December 1943, the 354th continued to perform this vital strategic role until after D-Day, when it reverted to Ninth Air Force control. Amongst the first Merlin-engined Mustangs seen in the UK, these two P-51B-5s of the 355th FS/354th FG are being fitted with 75-US gal tanks in preparation for a bomber escort mission in late 1943 (*via Michael O'Leary*)

# P-47 THUNDERBOLT PILOTS

## Lt Col Selden R Edner
## Executive Officer (Flying)
## 4th FG

### DEFENSIVE

1. Turn into an attack – timing is important here. You must not turn too early and again not too late. Try to turn when the Hun is just out of range.

2. If the Hun is diving for an attack and you turn a sharp 90 degrees right or left, he will usually try a full deflected shot and keep on going down. This is where you can immediately turn on his tail and catch him in the dive.

This photograph was taken at Debden in March 1943 by *Flight's* staff photographer during the official Press introduction to the Thunderbolt in the ETO. Assigned to the 4th FG's 334th FS, the aircraft carries full identification striping on the nose, fin/rudder and tailplane. Note the clutch of 'Fleet Street's finest' in front of P-47C-2 41-6209 (*via Aeroplane*)

This nondescript P-47C-2 was put through its paces for the benefit of the press gathered at Debden. Note the massive size of the underwing star and the yellow-outlined fuselage insignia. All three squadrons within the 4th FG had fully transitioned from the Spitfire to the Thunderbolt by the end of April 1943 (*via Michael O'Leary*)

The Duchess of Kent visited Debden on 24 June 1943 to bestow the Royal Badges of Nos 71, 121 and 133 Eagle Squadrons upon the corresponding 4th FG units (334th, 335th and 336th FSs) in the name of the King. Following the parade ground ceremony, the Duchess was shown a specially prepared, de-cowled, P-47C-2 at close quarters. This particular aircraft was the pride and joy of a S/Sgt Belcher, who can be seen anxiously observing proceedings from behind the official party (*via Dick Martin*)

Two future COs of the 335th FS enjoy the summer sun at Debden in mid-1943. At left is Leon Blanding, who was an ex-No 121 'Eagle' Sqn pilot that served two tours with the 4th FG between 1942-44. In the foreground is George 'Carp' Carpenter, also formerly of No 121 Sqn. He was CO of the 335th from 5 February to 18 April 1944, when he was shot down by an enemy aircraft over Germany and made a PoW. Carpenter had claimed 13.833 kills, one probable and eight damaged prior to his capture (*via Dick Martin*)

3. It is always advisable to break into the sun when being attacked, if the situation affords it. He can't very well follow you with that glare in his eyes.

If you're outnumbered, get into any cloud cover as soon as possible and go home. Remember to uncage your artificial horizon and directional gyro before going in.

4. Most American fighters today can out-dive the enemy. If you have altitude go flat out in about a 50-degree dive, not vertically.

If you're caught on the deck and cannot outrun the Hun, do stay and turn with him, trying to allow him only full deflection shots or head-on attacks. Here again you can turn a defensive manoeuvre into an offensive one.

5. I want a wingman to try and position himself to shoot down any Hun who I cannot deal with myself.

**OFFENSIVE**

1. The most frequent shots, I believe, come when enemy aircraft are attempting to attack the bombers. This can best be dealt with by catching the Hun when he is out of range of the bombers and meeting him head-on. He will not stay and face your fire, but will break off, giving you an opportunity to get on his tail.

This particular P-47C-2 was the mount of 335th FS CO (and future six-kill ace) Roy W Evans, although he did not claim any of his victories with it. Initially assigned to the 334th FS as 'white 06' on 16 January 1943, the fighter was passed on to the 335th FS on 17 March, where it remained until retired to 2906 Observation Training Group at Atcham on 20 September. Despite the fighter being assigned to Evans on 29 May, he scored his first Thunderbolt kills (in July and August) in D-1 42-7863 (*via Bill Hess*)

The final moments of an Fw 190, caught on the gun camera film of Capt Don Gentile's P-47D-5 42-8659 on 14 January 1944. The 336th FS pilot claimed a brace of Focke-Wulfs on this sortie, taking his score to 5.333, and giving him ace status (*via John Stanaway*)

This P-47D-1 was flown by the 334th FS's Lt Vic France. A native of Dallas, Texas, the ex-No 71 Sqn pilot was killed in action flying a P-51B on 18 April 1944 (*via Dick Martin*)

Never attempt to get on a Hun's tail who is headed for an attack on the bombers, unless you are sure of getting him before he arrives within shooting range of them. You are leaving yourself wide open to be shot at by your own friendly bombers.

2. The Hun will, 90 per cent of the time, try diving vertically or near vertically. However, today our own fighters can dive just a little faster, so go after him, but at the same time watch your own hind quarters.

3. If superior numbers of enemy aircraft are in a position where you can attack from above, by all means do it. Use your excess speed from the dive after the attack to regain altitude, turning and climbing into the sun when possible.

If the enemy aircraft are above you in superior numbers, get the hell out the shortest way possible.

### Selden Raymond Edner

Born on 26 January 1919 in Fergus Falls, Minnesota, Selden Edner moved to California in the 1930s and, after reading about the war in Europe, left home to join the Royal Canadian Air Force. After flight training, he was sent to Britain to join No 121 'Eagle' Sqn, and on 8 August 1941, whilst flying a Hurricane IIB, he shared in the probable destruction of a Ju 88 near Hull. The bomber was the unit's first victory claim. By the end of October No 121 Sqn had transitioned to the Spitfire, and Edner used the fighter to down an Fw 190 near St Omer, in France, on 15 April 1942. On 17 May he claimed another Focke-Wulf fighter in the same location, and on 31 July he destroyed two Bf 109Fs near Berck-sur-Mer. Finally, on 19 August he claimed another Fw 190 near Dieppe to become an ace.

When the three Eagle Squadrons transferred to the USAAF in September 1942, Edner was commissioned as a captain. On 29 April 1943 he achieved the rank of major, and by October he was with the 336th FS/4th FG. Promoted to lieutenant colonel on 29 November, Edner then assumed command of the 336th.

On 8 March 1944 Edner was forced down in his P-51B near Berlin and made a PoW. His final tally was 6.5 destroyed, one probable and two damaged. Following VE-Day, Edner was repatriated and remained in the post-war military, transferring to the regular army on 5 July 1946. On 21 January 1949 he was shot down by ground fire while flying a light aircraft near Karpenision, in Greece. Captured by communist guerrillas upon extricating himself from the wrecked aircraft, Edner was subsequently murdered by his captors.

One of the tallest pilots in the 4th FG, Lt Col Selden Edner poses with two unamed RAF fighter pilots at Debden in late 1943 (*via Tom Ivie*)

### COL HUBERT ZEMKE
### COMMANDING OFFICER
### 56th FG

A fighter pilot must possess an inner urge to do combat. The will at all times to be offensive will develop into his own tactics.

If the enemy is above, never let your speed drop below 200 mph indicated, and don't climb because you lose too much speed. Turn into him at a point when you can present a head-on target. This means the proper timing for an enemy who is making a long dive on you.

If you're attacked on the same level, remember you can out-climb the enemy at altitude. Do your climbing in a circle, not a straight line, so as always to present him with a deflection shot until you can put him at a disadvantage.

To turn the tables when attacked, put everything forward and twist and turn until you can get into a circle. Never reverse your turn. Sometimes as a last resort when you have plenty of altitude, you can make a diving turn to give you plenty of distance, recover going straight up to orient yourself, then roll straight up to go into a turning circle.

The sun can be used to get out of a defensive situation by pulling straight up into it and blinding your opponent. The sun seldom helps when first appearing over the horizon or just setting. Always try to launch an attack from out of the sun.

Beware of high thin cirrus clouds. The enemy can look down through them, but you can't look up through them. If flying home short of gasoline and not in a position to do combat, either fly just a foot above the cloud level or else 10,000 ft above it. An airplane is

This evocative image is one in a sequence of well known photographs featuring early 56th FG Thunderbolts that were taken by the press from a B-24 on 25 May 1943. This echelon down is led by 62nd FS Operations Officer Capt Horace Craig in his P-47D 42-7870/LM-R *PAPPY*. Next is P-47C 41-6224/LM-X *TWO ROLL CHARLIE*, which *was* assigned to Lt Conway Saux, then Capt Gene O'Neill's P-47C 41-6347/LM-O *LIL ABNER*, followed by Lt Robert Taylor's P-47C 41-6193/LM-B *GINGER* and Lt Robert Stover's P-47C 41-6209/LM-C. Cropped out of this particular shot is Lt Harry Coronios' P-47D 42-7860 *GREK*. Only Craig and O'Neill would survive hostilities (*via Michael O'Leary*)

picked up just over a cloud layer very easily and you either want to be in a position to nip in very fast or trust that you won't be picked up at all. Don't go weaving down through valleys of cumulus, either with a squadron or by yourself. The enemy can come dashing around a corner and be on your tail before you know it. When popping out of a cloud, always do a turn and look back. You may have jumped out directly in front of a gun barrel. Try never to pull contrails – they can be seen for miles.

When attacked by large numbers of enemy aircraft, immediately turn into them and meet them head on. In most cases, half of them will break up and go down. Handle those remaining in an all-out fight until you're down to one, then take him on.

When caught on the deck, the only thing to do is twist and kick the rudder and stay as low as possible. If the clouds are low (1000 ft or less), do a turning climb, wide open, up into them.

I try to attack always from the rear and slightly below, with plenty of closing speed. This means that I probably started from superior altitude, and out of the sun. Of late, the enemy has always been diving on bombers from above. I can usually see him roll over and I generally roll over and down to draw in back of him.

The enemy has, for the last four months primarily, tried to get away by out-diving us, although he can't touch the dive of the P-47. Just hold on and you will catch him. They are most prone to level out and slow down before entering clouds. This is a wonderful time to make them change their minds.

As often as not they will try to evade by going straight down in an aileron roll. Stay pretty well back and to the outside of the enemy and get him as soon as he recovers.

**It did not take long for pilots and crew chiefs of the 63rd FS/56th FG to discover that the huge sides of the P-47's fuselage made an ideal canvas for a wide variety of art. Here, Lt Joseph Egan poses with his suitably personalised P-47C 41-6584/ UN-E *HOLY JOE*. This aircraft was written off after a crash-landing on 1 December 1943, whilst Egan (a five-victory ace) was killed when his P-47D-25 (42-26524) was shot down by flak near Nancy on 19 July 1944. He had just returned to the ETO to start his second tour, having been promoted to lead the 63rd FS. Egan's command of the unit lasted just 48 hours (*via Michael O'Leary*)**

63rd FS/56th FG P-47C-5 41-6537/ UN-Q was the mount of Lt Wilfred Van Abel, who subsequently went missing in this aircraft over Occupied Europe on 2 September 1943, although he survived as a prisoner. Standing on the wing of the fighter is its Crew Chief, Sgt Damon Itza, who was later selected to look after 'Hub' Zemke's Thunderbolt when the CO of the 56th FG moved it from the 62nd to the 63rd FS in September 1943. The artwork worn by this P-47 was inspired by the squadron's 'Gus the Gunner' emblem (*via Michael O'Leary*)

Sometimes the enemy will spin down. Remember, they must recover. Keep superior altitude and always have your kite under control.

The greater the number of the enemy, the harder one has to hit them to break them up. For instance, suppose you saw three Fws below some 2000 or 3000 ft. This is the ideal occasion when you could drift down at a good clip, devoting most of your attention to one and polishing him off. Now, if there were 20 down below, you'd probably come screaming down with full force to pick out the most logical enemy aircraft at the point of firing, then pull up immediately to a good altitude and develop another attack on one of those remaining who has been shaken out of his helmet by your sudden onslaught.

When by yourself, and seeing two or more enemy aircraft above, move away to get superior position and then attack. When you have your outfit with you and the enemy has so much altitude that you'd never get to him, just stay below and in the rear of him. He'll be down.

I have never yet cut my throttle just to hang on the tail of an enemy aircraft. I always move past him, going just about straight up. You'll always win a battle as long as you can stay above. Take him on the next try. The idea of cutting the throttle, as so often heard, to allow the enemy to pass has never appealed to me. They're too good at gunnery.

I stay with an enemy until: he's destroyed; I'm out of ammunition; he evades into the clouds; I'm driven off; or I'm too low on gasoline to continue the combat.

In attacking, I like my wingman about 500 to 1000 ft above and to the side. At low altitudes more. On a co-ordinated attack into a formation he should be off to the side 500 ft and just a bit back.

Never fire at anything more than 30 degrees off the line of flight unless you just want to scare him. As yet I haven't hit an enemy

aircraft moving straight down or while in a slow or half roll. Always hold your fire until the enemy has filled the 300-yard sight bar. The point stressed here is to fight for a kill position and then fire.

Always break off the attack upward and into the sun. Look back and up immediately because you might have another fight on your hands. Recover in a circular climb.

Our formations are maintained in two different ways. For the purpose of climbing to the enemy coast, the entire group flies in very close – that is, each squadron. Each flight of four aircraft flies in a close four-airplane Vee. The number two man has the option of taking whatever side he desires, then the three and four men take the other side. The next flight should be within 50 yards or less, depending on the comfort to the particular flight leader, and whether or not there is good or bad visibility. By flying close in this way, a great deal of formation jockeying is avoided.

Just before enemy territory is reached, the order 'Battle Formation' is given, and this same four aircraft Vee formation is extended on a front of approximately 200 to 300 yards. The second flight is then on either the left or right flank (the sun has a bearing on this, of course) and above some 500 ft. This same formation is employed on escort after rendezvous.

The front type formation is superior to string formation in that it prevents any enemy attack without it being seen. Remember, few pilots are shot down by enemies they see. It is also a search formation.

Upon contacting a bomber force, I give my squadrons' disposition. On penetration, I usually place myself so that I can roam with one squadron several miles in front, while the other two squadrons are stationed one on either flank. If the bomber force is more than two

The 63rd FS's Lt Wayne O'Connor with his dog 'Slipstream' on his P-47C-2 41-6216/UN-O, which boasted a big bad wolf insignia. This aircraft was lost whilst being flown by another squadron pilot on 19 August 1943, whilst O'Connor was shot down and killed on 11 November 1943 (*via Michael O'Leary*)

combat wings, then the squadrons are split from the group and each is assigned a combat wing. There they remain. Withdrawal support is no different other than the fact that the squadron which I normally put out in front is placed in back, or to wander at random, assisting straggling bombers or wherever the help is most needed.

A squadron of 16 fighters is self-sustaining, the four flights of four aircraft each making up the four basic units of the squadron. When escorting, two flights, or eight aircraft, patrol below looking for action while the remaining two flights stay 1000 ft above to make sure the lower eight are not molested. If a 12-airplane squadron is used, then only one flight gives this top cover.

By assigning the squadrons definite positions, and requiring them to remain on their assignments, I, as well as the other members of the group, pretty well know where the others are. Of course, this may mean that squadrons are sometimes five or ten miles apart, and not in visual contact, but it permits us to sweep a very large area. Flights within the squadron never move more than a mile apart, and are always within very good visual reference.

In the above situation, if one squadron is engaged in a heavy fight, the other two squadrons rush over to give top cover and pick off the disorganised enemy.

Each squadron will range from the bombers sometimes two or three miles as they orbit along the bomber course, but seldom so far that a fighter in the vicinity of the bombers cannot be immediately identified. Never drop your speed below 200 mph indicated, so you can bounce fast.

Flights must be dependent upon the main flight of the squadron commander unless the fighting is extremely heavy. Any flight may bounce, but it must first call the enemy in and allow the squadron commander to see if he can't pick up the target. If he can't see it, then he immediately says 'Go get them' and gives the junior flight top cover.

As to limitations on bounce, this must be remembered – the ones and threes of the flights are the only outright firing men. The twos and fours are cover men, who look to see their leaders are not being attacked as they concentrate on the enemy. Under only one circumstance will number twos and number fours break away to make an attack, and that is when the flight leader can't find the target. He should immediately say 'Go get them' and take a number two position himself, assuming the role of coverage. This same holds true as to squadron commanders calling in the enemy to a group commander – I speak here only of the offensive. On the defensive, fire whenever you can.

Flights generally fly from 200 to 300 yards apart at all times after the battle formation order is given. The battle will spread them wide open soon enough.

Reforming at altitude is always a problem, but two general practices have worked quite successfully. After an engagement the squadron commander will call his outfit to form up in the same position on the bombers they had before, and then everyone heads for that point. The squadron commander will do slow rolls, wag his wings or form his

**One of the most successful fighter leaders of all time, Hubert 'Hub' Zemke commanded the 56th FG for almost two years. Here, he is seen posing in front of a 61st FS P-47C during the summer of 1943** (*352nd FG Association*)

flight in a diamond to show the others his position. Another method is to pick a town or landmark below and have everyone circle up, reforming over this point. The order will be given for all to circle in a right turn, for instance, to prevent confusion. All turning in other directions are enemy.

I have tried the 24-aircraft group on deep penetration and find this to be the most self-sustaining fighting force yet – organised in three eight-aircraft squadrons – not two 12s. By ranging over a wider area we can find the enemy more easily than when in a small compact area.

Never despatch the entire outfit to engage an inferior number of attacking aircraft. Everyone will become disorganised in the break and the following melee if all are used. If one squadron is overcome, then despatch another squadron. The fight will be below you and you shouldn't have much difficulty. Don't be drawn away from your outfit, but hover as top cover.

It must be realised that a group flying properly together presents a front which prevents all parts from being attacked at the same time. Someone can always offer cover.

Learn to break at the proper time to make a head-on attack. The enemy doesn't like it. Don't run. That's just what he wants you to do. He can't help from getting right behind you if you are moving away. When caught by the enemy in large force the best policy is to fight like hell until you can decide what to do next.

The size of the enemy force must be extremely large and you with only a flight to do anything other than break and break and break. Take an occasional squirt to scare them or try and hit them as they pass.

Whenever the enemy is within yours or his own striking distance, drop your belly tank. Only one exception to the rule presents itself to me and that is to drop your tanks if he is in large numbers well above, even though out of striking range.

Often times the enemy pilots peel down past you just to suck you down, so that others still above can get down on you. Waiting for the last men to come down is generally the correct thing to do. Don't pass up the tail end of a formation to get the leader.

As group and squadron leader, I always take a bounce first, unless there are so many of the enemy that help is needed. In that case I say, 'You take such and such and I will take this one'.

I always take down four to one against four enemy aircraft. There are only two offensive firers in each flight. This always keeps a flight together and provides a ratio of two firers for us against one of them. If they are superior in numbers, then the order is just 'Everybody follow me'. I never lead down the entire group on such an occasion, only a squadron. Once an attack is launched you should not give up until the enemy is destroyed.

Meet the enemy at any and all angles, preferably head on, and in nine cases out of ten he won't get a chance to fire at the bombers. Your next pass at the same fellow, or perhaps that one, will bring him down. Always launch the attack – don't wait around. Hesitant pilots seldom bring home the bacon. Once you make a decision or give an order, follow through, otherwise you will only confuse others.

Forever impress on your juniors the Huns they lost. A record is never established by the ones that got away. Everyone is most prone to let the tougher ones get away, yet it is found that one reaps only the benefit of his own aggressiveness. Fighting is developing your own breaks.

Flight and element leaders have all the liberty a leader can allow to initiate a bounce. However, it must be realised that a squadron or group leader cannot allow his organisation to peel off at random for bounces. Leaders would find themselves without much control. Therefore, it is a policy to identify both yourself and the bogie or bandit. The squadron or group leader tries to find the enemy, and if he doesn't succeed, will give the order for the flight or element leader to attack and will give cover himself.

## Hubert 'Hub' Zemke

Another official US Army Air Forces photograph of Col 'Hub' Zemke, taken at the same time as the shot on page 21. He has donned his much prized RAF 'C' Type flying helmet, complete with B-7 goggles, for this photo (*via I J Phillips*)

Born on 14 March 1914 in Missoula, Montana, Hubert Zemke was of German ancestry. Going on to attend Montana State University, he left his studies six months short of graduation to join the Army Reserves as a flying cadet in February 1936, and was rated an AP on 17 February 1937 at Kelly Field, in Texas. He was assigned to the 36PS/8th PG, and was rated as a pilot on 15 August 1939. Becoming a first lieutenant on 9 September 1940, Zemke's next assignment was the 56th PG's Headquarters Squadron on 22 May 1941. With the start of the war promotions were rapid, and he became a captain on 1 February 1942 and a major on 1 March of the same year!

When hostilities commenced in Europe, Zemke was sent to Britain to act as an observer and then to Russia as a military air attaché, where he taught Russian pilots how to fly their new P-40s. By September 1942 Zemke had become commanding officer of the 56th FG, and he duly led the group to Britain in December of the same year. He scored his first confirmed victory on 14 May 1943 when he damaged a Fw 190 near Antwerp, in Belgium, and achieved ace status on 2 October that same year.

By August 1944 Zemke had been credited with 15.25 victories (out of a total of 665 kills achieved by the 56th, which had become known as 'Zemke's Wolfpack'). He was then transferred to take command of the 479th FG, forsaking the P-47 for the P-51. Whilst leading his new group he ran into a violent storm over Germany on 30 October 1944 that forced him to bail out of his fighter. Zemke was quickly captured by the Germans and transferred to *Stalag Luft I*, where he remained until war's end.

Following repatriation, he stayed in the USAF and served in a variety of commands before retiring as a colonel on 31 July 1966. 'Hub' Zemke died in California on 30 August 1994 after contracting pneumonia. His final tally was 17.75 confirmed, two probables and nine damaged.

# Lt Col David C Schilling
# Executive Officer (Flying)
# 56th FG

I feel it a privilege to write to you of what little knowledge of fighter tactics I have been fortunate enough to attain during my present tour of operational duty. I am not going to attempt to answer your questions by number, but rather write a short narrative on each phase as you have outlined in your letter to me. It must be remembered that everyone indulges in his own intricacies and, even though to himself they more or less afford the desired ends, they may not be satisfactory for others. Bearing this in mind, I will do my best.

The age old adage 'that a good offensive is a good defence' holds true nearly every time. No matter how offensive an individual or group of pilots is, when outnumbered, they will at one time or another get an enemy aircraft behind them. The only good evasive action is a tight turning circle, and if that doesn't put you on your opponent's tail or cause him to break or spiral down, then a series of diving aileron rolls until sufficient speed is built up to pull away will usually get you to safety. Once on the deck, if still pursued, skidding and 'jinking' of the aircraft is the only thing to do. One must bear in mind that flying right on the treetops is not satisfactory, as there is too great a danger of collision with ground objects, and the extra ten or twenty feet of proximity to the ground does not help enough to warrant the chance mentioned above.

When attacked, a break at the right time will cause the enemy to make a very high deflection shot and sometimes overshoot to allow

Executive Officer of the 56th FG, Maj David Schilling (left), receives a handshake from 63rd FS CO, Maj Sylvester Burke, upon returning from the successful mission of 4 October 1943. On this day, the 56th FG had provided part of the penetration escort for B-17s sent to bomb targets in Frankfurt. As the 'heavies' approached the target, a formation of twin-engined Bf 110s was spotted preparing to attack the rear Fortress formations near Duren. Led by Schilling (in P-47C-5 41-6347), the 63rd FS fell on the enemy, shooting down 14 Messerschmitt heavy fighters – a record score for a USAAF squadron up to that point in the war. The total credited to the 56th FG as a whole was 16 aircraft destroyed. Schilling claimed a solitary Bf 110, taking his tally to three. By 10 October he had boosted his score to five, making him an ace. Behind Schilling and Burke are other pilots who participated in the 4 October 'Messerschmitt Massacre' (*via Michael O'Leary*)

Coming home over the cold cruel North Sea. P-47C 41-6385/HV-Y was first assigned to Lt Robill Roberts, but in December 1943 Claude Mussey took it over. Following his loss over the North Sea in March 1944, the fighter passed into general use, before being retired to the 495th Fighter Training Group in May 1944 – by which time it was the last P-47C in service with the 56th FG (*via Sam Sox*)

you to pull into an astern position on him. Never break upwards but on the same level, because breaking upwards causes a loss of speed and affords an easier target for the enemy. If necessary to pull up into an attack, hold it until the enemy aircraft is in a head-on position, then do so and fire. Incidentally, I believe that on a head-on shot 'he who shoots first lives'. You don't stand a very good chance of hitting anything, but it frightens your opponent and shakes his aim.

The few times we have been hit by a superior number of aircraft, we got several turning circles going with enemy aircraft interspersed in the circle. If you work hard and do a lot of snap shooting, you can usually scare a lot of them out until you can get them whittled down to your size, and then you can bait them by having one element lessen its rate of turn, watching not to let the enemy close up or be able to pull enough deflection so that the second element can then close up and get into proper position to fire. Usually after several have been destroyed in this manner, the rest will become discouraged and break for the deck, and can be pursued and shot down if everyone is on his toes.

Two things to always remember in combat are:

1. The only time to do any sloppy flying is when someone is firing at you, and then if uncoordinated flying is necessary for evasive action, really get sloppy.

2. Always assume that the enemy is in the sun or clouds above.

When launching an attack, always clear the sky above and particularly the sun. The number attacked makes no difference – attack anyway, but if you are alone or only have two ships, take the rear or side of the enemy formation. If you have a flight, as a leader always attack farther up the formation to allow a good chance for your second element leader. If you have a squadron of 12 or 16, always attack the front portion of the formation by diving below and climbing up from the rear on the front aeroplanes. When doing this, the entire squadron has to be spread out in such a manner as to enable everyone to fire simultaneously. This is a ticklish thing for the leader to get set

up, and involves excellent timing, surprise, good initial position, and a high rate of speed. Such a case does not often occur, but when it does, every effort should be made to make a clean co-ordinated attack, otherwise someone is liable to get badly shot up and only a few of the enemy aircraft will be destroyed.

When attacking individually or with a wingman, the general success is usually dependent on the element of surprise. On a bounce that is a long distance below, a very loose wing-over with power partially cut will reduce your speed and consequent rate of closure, which will allow more time for trimming, sighting and shooting. I personally prefer to come out of my dive several hundred feet below the enemy aircraft so that I will not be so easily detected. I always prefer that my wingman fly well up so that he can fire if I miss my target.

The number of aeroplanes that are sent down on a bounce is determined by the number of aircraft to be attacked. If the enemy aircraft outnumber our formation and we are certain that no aircraft are in the vicinity above, we send every available aeroplane down for one simultaneous effort or by rapid succession of flights, the last flight covering the first flight and likewise as the last flight goes in, the first flight pulling up covers the last. If the general area is somewhat infested with pairs or small numbers of enemy aircraft, we then always leave one flight up for cover to bounce anything that might come in on the attacking flight's tail.

**Quite often when escort missions were completed Thunderbolt pilots would head for the deck and hit German targets – a task decidedly more hazardous than tangling with Luftwaffe fighters. Whilst hosing down a flak tower at Chartres with his eight 0.50-cal machine guns on 17 March 1944, the pilot of the Thunderbolt that took this photograph with his gun camera almost shot down his element leader when he turned in front of him. Note how well the wide identification bands stand out from the Olive Drab camouflage (*via Michael O'Leary*)**

My method of firing is definitely not very good, and I find that my estimation of angle off is usually always in error on the underside. Therefore, I am very careful to get a good line of sight and purposely over allow from three-fourths to one-half a ring more deflection than I think is necessary. I then decrease my lead slowly until I see strikes. I then increase my lead to the point when the sight is in the same position as it was just prior to the time I saw strikes. This usually gives me a heavy concentration of strikes and achieves the desired ends. I break off my attack with a sharp climbing turn and recover into the sun.

The only reason for failure to attack enemy aircraft is a fuel shortage. If for any reason it is believed that your combat will carry you to a low altitude where it will be necessary for an extended period of combat, or a race home on the deck, don't attack if you have not sufficient fuel to carry out your plans.

The group always flies with the three squadrons in a 'V', with the lead squadron in the centre, the down-sun squadron from 800 to 1000 ft above, and the up-sun squadron from 1000 to 1500 ft above the group leader. To the enemy coast the flights are flown in a very compact formation, and the three squadrons together never form a formation more than a mile wide and 200 to 300 yards long. This keeps the group as one unit, and prevents mixing with other friendly units if encountered on the way in. At the enemy coast the squadrons slide out so that the lead ships of each squadron are approximately one half-mile out from the lead squadron. The flights fly line abreast so that the group appears as a flat 'V', or jagged line, 36 to 48 ships across. This formation is held until the escort is begun, then two flights fly in a staggered string, one flight slightly back and the third approximately 1000 ft above for top cover.

It is highly desirable that flights fly approximately one half-mile or slightly less apart, and try as much as possible to stay in supporting distance because many times this has saved members of an engaged flight that was attacked, and resulted in higher scores and lower losses. Also in an extended formation, if an attack is made on them, only one section of it is placed on the defensive rather than the entire section. This then allows the remainder to become offensive and drive off the attackers.

Flights bounce independently on initial engagements after informing the squadron or group leader, if the latter is in the immediate vicinity. Elements never attack without the flight leader's permission unless as a result of combat they have become detached and are operating on their own. Under no circumstances does a wingman ever leave for a bounce unless his leader orders him to do so. After very heavy engagements the squadrons always reform on the flank of the bomber formation that they are briefed to escort.

The squadrons are always assigned the same positions for every mission, that is, the 61st Squadron on the left, the 62nd Squadron on the right, and the 63rd Squadron well out ahead. if the bomber formation is considerable strung out, the 61st Squadron is assigned the rear, the 62nd Squadron the second box and the 63rd Squadron the lead box. To reform, the command is given by the squadron leader or the group commander, and everyone orbits left in the assigned area and as quickly as possible forms four-ship flights with no regard for who leads what. The main object is to get a formation together and to get it identified and resume escort.

There has been much controversy as to how far to leave the bombers to attack or search for enemy aircraft. If there is no enemy action near the bombers, the lead squadron pulls out ahead eight or ten miles and searches. The days of our highest scores have always been in the immediate vicinity of the bombers. Sometimes we have to go to very low altitudes to press home the attack, but the recovery is always made below the bombers, and doesn't take the element or flight away for very long.

On several occasions the rumour has been spread that we left the bombers entirely and went down to 10,000 ft or below and engaged enemy aircraft and came home. We have, but because there were large numbers beneath the bombers, climbing and waiting for us to leave. At the time the bombers were not under attack and our fuel was getting very low. If we could disperse and destroy them before we were forced to withdraw, we would indirectly aid the bombers by preventing attack after we would normally leave. There is no set thumb rule as to how far you can leave the bombers because the tactics and the strategy of the situation are mentally weighed and thought out on the scene of the engagement, and can never be predicted prior to a mission.

I can sum it up in saying that the main object of every fighter group should be to, if possible, avoid all engagements prior to rendezvous, and upon rendezvous never, if possible, leave the bombers without escort or support unless driven off by enemy attacks.

In closing, I wish to state that being on the offensive all of the time and attacking (although more than normal risk is involved) will give a group higher scores and lower losses in any engagement, because aggressiveness on our part shakes the enemy to such a degree that he becomes excited and discouraged.

## POSTSCRIPT

Since I wrote my last letter, the group has run into somewhat different enemy tactics, particularly so on the Berlin shows. On penetration, I feel it highly advisable to concentrate all the strength on the front box. The enemy usually sends in waves of eight to twelve for frontal attacks, separated by 45 seconds to a minute-and-a-half. After we use a 12-ship squadron to break up the first effort, the second for the second, and so on, the first cannot recover and reform soon enough to break up the fourth effort, if any. Therefore, we like to have both groups, A and B, well up to the front, with one group 2000 ft above and in the sun standing by to come in after the first group gets fought out of position. This will allow the first group to re-position itself and do the same for the second if necessary.

For the first portion of the enemy attack no one should go below 5000 ft beneath the bombers because it takes them too far from the bombers to give them any further support. After all the initial attacks have been attempted and they are reforming for a second try, then is the time to press home the attack, but leave at least two squadrons or one group to prevent any second wave, if any.

## David Carl Schilling

Born on 15 December 1918 in the army town of Leavenworth, Kansas, Dave Schilling would go on to attend prestigious Dartmouth College, graduating in 1939. Soon after he joined the army, enlisting as a flying cadet, and then went on to become commissioned as a second lieutenant on 11 May 1940 at Brooks Field in Texas. Originally assigned to the newly-formed 56th PG in June 1941, he soon went to the 63rd PS (pursuit groups and squadrons became fighter groups and squadrons in May 1942). Here, he initially flew P-40Es.

With the start of the war, Schilling was soon promoted, and he had made captain by 1 March 1942, and was later given command officer of the 62nd FS. In June of that year the 56th FG received P-47Bs in advance of its move to Britain. The group arrived in the ETO in December-January, and Schilling flew his first combat mission during April 1943. He achieved ace status in early October, and by mid-August 1944 had become the 56th FG's commanding officer. Promoted to full colonel, Schilling held this position until 27 January 1945. By the end of the war, he had flown 132 combat missions and claimed 22.5 kills.

A career officer, Schilling stayed in the post-war air force and assumed, once again, command of the 56th FG on 24 April 1946. By this time, the group was based at Selfridge Field, in Michigan, and converting to the new P-80 Shooting Star. On 7 July 1948, he led the 56th on an epic flight to Furstenfeldbruck airfield, in Berlin, returning two weeks later to establish the feasibility of jet fighter ferry flights across the Atlantic. Two years later, on 22 September 1950, he piloted a modified Republic F-84 from London to Bangor, Maine, in just over ten hours – a trip that required air-to-air refuelling on three occasions. Throughout his career, Schilling would continue to perform pioneering jet flights, as well as advancing in rank, until his untimely death on 14 August 1956 in a car accident in Suffolk, England. His final victory tally was 22.5 confirmed destroyed and six damaged.

Maj Dave Schilling poses for the camera just prior to climbing aboard Col 'Hub' Zemke's P-47C-5 41-6330 *MOY TOVARISH* at Horsham St Faith in the summer of 1943 (*via Bill Hess*)

## Lt Col Horace C Craig
## 56th FG

In reply to your letter I submit the following informal brief of combat tactics which are in every respect very general and have been published in different forms many times previous. I can only discuss tactics as I encountered them, which are only my own views and are open to the criticism of others.

As an introductory statement, I trained several small units of new pilots after I completed my tour and noticed that their training had lacked discipline as soldiers as well as air discipline. I make such a statement on the grounds that new pilots should 'listen' and ask questions to try to learn, instead of starting to dictate after a mission or two. When not training or flying actual combat, new pilots should be learning their equipment and constantly maintaining a higher standard of proficiency, rather than the lackadaisical attitude which can so easily jeopardise the efficiency of a combat organisation.

Before answering your individual questions, I will make a brief summary of our formation and tactics, as they differ greatly in every unit.

Our take-offs were in ships of twos, using two runways for quicker scrambles. Immediately the flights of fours closed in to a Vickers V formation, and the flights as well closed in to three Vickers V formations to form the squadrons which orbited to the desired altitude in this manner, and on into enemy-occupied territory. This type of formation is manoeuvrable and very good for bad weather flying, saving fuel, prevention of accidents and keeping compact formation.

As the group set course for enemy territory, the squadrons kept well abreast and about a mile apart slightly above the lead squadron. When the group reached enemy-occupied territory, the group leader gave the signal for battle formation, which spread the squadrons slightly out, and the flights out 600 to 800 yards. Each man in the flight stacked out to the sides and not dead astern, so the flight leaders can keep an accurate check on each ship. This battle formation is maintained at all times over enemy territory and until a safe distance from home bases, with each man constantly on the alert.

Now to follow your letter and make a statement to each question as to how I would do it, and to add any further comment I might think useful at the end of this letter.

Horace 'Pappy' Craig commanded the 56th FG's 62nd FS from mid-August 1943 through to early the following year. On 3 February Craig passed the 200-hour mark in operational flying, which at the time was the established point when a fighter pilot was to be rested. The first man within the 56th to complete a tour, Craig flew some 80 missions during his nine months in the ETO. Throughout this time he was presented with the opportunity to shoot down an enemy aircraft just once – on 20 December 1943 he claimed a Do 217 bomber destroyed (*via I J Phillips*)

## DEFENSIVE

When attacked by enemy aircraft, the main objective is to break into the attacking aircraft and get on the offensive immediately. To stay on the defensive means defeat to part or all of the formation, so I would climb the formation, trying for every advantage to gain a point where a successful attack could be launched. Once a turn is started in an engagement, it is of the most importance, and safety of the individual pilot, to remember to *never reverse your turn*.

It has been my observation that a great majority of the victories of my unit were made good when the Hun reversed the turn, allowing an attack to be made from dead astern without the slightest deflection. When attacked always be aggressive, and if decidedly outnumbered and the offensive cannot be gained, I would then, and then only, hit the deck for home.

In any engagements, offensive or defensive, take advantage of favourable conditions – clouds, sun, etc. Launch your attacks from up-sun, when the enemy aircraft least expect it, if possible. Your position, and the element of surprise, initiated during the attack, mean everything. Never allow yourself or your formation to be placed in such a position that you do not have at least one sure plan of withdrawal.

When engaging vastly superior numbers, do so with as many aeroplanes as possible, and remain on the offensive with plenty of aggressiveness. When you lack offensive aggressiveness, get out in as compact a formation as possible until you can gain an advantage point. It is my estimate that one friendly aeroplane operating against the enemy can be of more value later when you have the advantage, rather than not admit defeat and lose several aeroplanes foolishly against superior equipment, or odds, in one particular combat.

If caught on the deck get as many objects between you and the attacking enemy aircraft with as much speed as possible, always flying in the direction of your home base.

## OFFENSIVE

When on the offensive, use every element in your favour against the enemy for as long as possible. To say the least, be aggressive at all times.

During an attack, have your men stacked out to the sides so you can account for every aeroplane. Wingmen are definitely to be used only to cover their leader's tail. Place your formation to block and attack ever possible means of escape available to the enemy aircraft, making sure you are not being tricked. The common trick of the Hun – to place a decoy with a main force still in the sun – has worked on numerous occasions with men who bounced first and looked afterwards. If you have sufficient aeroplanes available, take care of the decoy. Otherwise, manoeuvre into position to attack the main body and let the decoy go.

It is useless to fire great deflection bursts. Manoeuvre and orbit until you are certain not to overshoot the enemy aircraft, and so you can get a dead astern shot at the proper range. The closer the better! Only engage the enemy when you have a definite picture of the present surroundings and aircraft that can participate in that particular battle. When you lose the advantage, break away before you lose your

The legendary Francis 'Gabby' Gabreski emerged as the top US fighter ace in the ETO, scoring 28 aerial victories (he claimed a further 6.5 MiG kills flying F-86 Sabres with the 51st FIW during the Korean War). Having flown at least nine different P-47s during the course of his long career with the 56th FG, 'Gabby's' tally would have undoubtedly been higher had he not struck the ground with the propeller of P-47D-25 42-26418 while strafing He 111s at Bassinheim airfield on 20 July 1944. Managing to clear the target area, Gabreski successfully bellied the aircraft into a nearby field and was quickly captured (*Mighty Eighth HM*)

formation and always break into the sun straight up. There may be aeroplanes there you did not see, and you can cover all the other areas fairly well. After the attack be sure to join, regardless of your rank or position, the largest number of friendly aircraft so that you can still withdraw to the force and help others who are less fortunate. Never allow yourself or your formation to become scattered over too large an area.

The attack should be launched by the leaders of the formations or flight leaders. For any man just to peel out of the formation and attack is foolhardy! Always announce your intentions so the remainder of the formation can give cover, as you are briefed and trained to do.

It is a bad practice to engage enemy aircraft while still carrying belly tanks, or to keep the tanks when an attack is about to be launched against you. In my opinion, tanks should be released when exhausted (circumstances may make different action mandatory.)

It is the duty of the individual pilot to know his geographic features very well, and other military maps, in case there are adverse conditions and he is forced to return alone. The individual pilot should know his equipment so that he can get the best efficiency, endurance, speeds, etc. Never ditch a fighter-type aeroplane. Bail out, especially over water. Over the friendly coast, if possible, try a belly landing.

Last of all, and a most important factor, is the use of the radio transmitter. Know exactly what you are going to say before you press the button, and know when and which button to press. If you are in command and give an order, *do so with assurance*, so that you do not convey to others that you are not master of the situation. If it is wrong, go through with it. That is better than changing horses in the middle of the stream. Call in only aircraft that you can identify as ones that appear to be enemy within attacking range. Never cut others out on the radio transmitter, for neither of you have accomplished anything. Most important of all, *give the radio transmitter to the pilot who is actually engaged and needs it* – you may save his life. Remember, it could be you!

In conclusion, I advise each individual pilot to keep trying to maintain a higher standard of proficiency at all times. When you get too good to learn and listen to experience, you will soon meet with someone who is just a little better – and he is always present, no matter what the task.

## MAJ GERALD W JOHNSON
## COMMANDING OFFICER
## 63rd FS/56TH FG

There isn't a subject that I enjoy talking about and discussing with my pilots more than combat flying and tactics. However, my attempt to get these ideas on paper may not be too successful.

As a start I would like to say that early in my career as an active fighter pilot, my flight was attacked from the rear by 12 single-engined enemy aircraft. As a result of our defensive action on that occasion, two of our aircraft were badly shot up but returned to base. We realised then that our tactics were not right, so we got to work to find a system of defensive and offensive action that would work under any condition. It didn't take long to find the answer, and since then I have never been worried about being attacked.

The answer was this – never let yourself get in a defensive position. We will assume that you have seen the attack coming because, in my opinion, there is no excuse for not seeing it. If you make a very tight climbing turn in the direction they are coming from when they are still well out of firing range, and meet them as nearly head-on as possible, they will seldom continue the attack but will split up, breaking either up or down, and leaving you in a favourable position to pursue them.

However, if the enemy has slipped in on your tail to close range before you see him, your best action is to break down in as rough and erratic manoeuvres as you possibly can, and in the direction closest to

the enemy. In the case of a flight, each aeroplane in the flight should break individually as described above. If the enemy follows one of your aeroplanes, then the rest of the flight can recover and knock him off the unlucky pilot's tail. In my experience, this action has never failed to work. I would never go all the way to the deck as a defensive move unless I was greatly outnumbered and my only means of escape was by outrunning the enemy.

A wingman's job is definitely to stay with his leader at all times, searching the sky to the rear and above for enemy aircraft. When an attack is made he should follow his leader about 300 to 400 yards behind and out to the side, taking care of anything that might come down on them while in the attack. His only opportunity to shoot comes when his leader overshoots his target before it is destroyed.

Twenty-five-year-old Kentucky quail shooter Capt Gerald W Johnson was proclaimed the first ace of the 56th FG in August 1943. Considered one of his most able pilots by his CO, Col Zemke, Gerry Johnson eventually amassed a total of 16.5 aerial victories before being shot down by ground fire and made a PoW. In later years he rose to the rank of lieutenant general in the USAF, and commanded the Eighth Air Force during the Vietnam war. He is seen here with his ring spanner-wielding crew chief in early 1944 (*via Tom Ivie*)

It is my opinion that the element of surprise when making an attack is the greatest advantage that you can have. Most attacks are made from above and should definitely be planned so that you know before starting down that you will close on the enemy from such a position that you will destroy him, that you know how you will recover from the attack to give yourself the greatest advantage and safety in climbing back up, and to make it as easy as possible for your flight to stay with you. Once you have started an attack and have gone down quite a distance to get to the target, you should stay with him until he is destroyed, otherwise you have sacrificed your altitude and speed without accomplishing anything.

If you plan your attack right the enemy will seldom see you coming until you open fire. Therefore, you should hold your fire until you are in very close range, and then make that first burst really count. Because there might be something behind me, I always break off an attack in a very violent climbing turn.

I am very much in favour of a very tight four-ship V formation within the flights, and of the squadrons flying close to the lead squadron until the enemy coast is reached. Then spread out into a fairly tight battle formation, just enough to allow everyone to look around until rendezvous is made. A tight formation until the coast is reached is very good training – you can keep the group in a compact unit, and the pilots will tend to feel more free and will look around more when they go into battle formation.

The reasons for a semi-tight battle formation from the coast to rendezvous are that the group can stay together better, and a few enemy aeroplanes will hesitate to attack a large formation flying in good position. In the case of four flights per squadron, two flights should fly in line abreast, with the other two in line abreast slightly back and 500 to 1000 ft above. Within a flight the aeroplanes should be as nearly line abreast as possible.

Each squadron should be assigned a definite position in relation to the bombers. This makes it much easier to keep a squadron together,

In the age old fighter pilot's tradition of debriefing with his hands, this anonymous individual from the 56th FG graphically recounts his experiences to his groundcrew just minutes after returning from an escort mission over Germany (*via Michael O'Leary*)

and after a fight in which the squadron becomes separated, everyone will know where to return in order to find his squadron.

I believe the best formation while escorting is to have the flights fly astern of each other, and with about 400 yards between them. Then when the squadron orbits, each flight can protect the tail of the flight in front of them. Every flight leader should be given the privilege of attacking anything that he may see. I think that after you are in the battle area, a looser and more flexible formation will get more victories, because less time is spent in flying formation and each pilot has an opportunity to see more.

Developing among your pilots an aggressive spirit and a desire to fight and destroy the enemy will go a long way toward making a successful fighter outfit.

I feel that I have not covered this subject very thoroughly, but I hope that something I have said may be useful to someone.

## Gerald Walter 'Gerry' Johnson

Born on 10 July 1919 in Owenton, Kentucky, Johnson would go on to attend college, but left to enter the aviation cadet training programme in September 1941. Commissioned as a second lieutenant in April 1942, the new pilot was assigned to the 56th FG's 61st FS at Mitchell Field, in New York, where he flew a variety of aircraft including P-36s, P-40s and P-38s. Upon the group's transfer to Bridgeport, Connecticut, he received training on the first Republic P-47 Thunderbolts assigned to a frontline unit.

Shipped overseas, the group soon went into action as part of the Eighth Air Force in England. Johnson damaged an Fw 190 on 14 May 1943 near Antwerp, and followed this up with a confirmed victory on 26 June over an Fw 190 near Dieppe. From that point, his score began to rapidly rise. On 29 November 1943 he was transferred to the 360th FG in order to aid the unit's transition into combat. While flying with this group Johnson downed an Fw 190 on 24 January 1944. He duly returned to the 56th FG and became commander of the 63rd FS, with whom he claimed a further seven enemy aircraft. On 27 March 1944 he was himself struck down by anti-aircraft fire while strafing a train.

Quickly captured, Johnson remained a PoW until May 1945. He then returned to command the 56th FG at Selfridge Field, Michigan. He remained in the USAF and rapidly rose in rank, becoming a brigadier-general on 1 November 1965. As a lieutenant-general, Johnson was commander of the Eighth Air Force during the final three years of the Vietnam War. He retired as Inspector General of the USAF during September 1974. Johnson's final tally was 16.5 confirmed kills, one probable and 4.5 damaged.

The successful pilots within the 56th FG in 1943/44 were amongst the most photographed of all US aces during World War 2. This shot of Gerry Johnson was taken just days before he was downed by small arms fire whilst strafing targets in France (*via I J Phillips*)

# MAJ WALKER M MAHURIN
## 63rd FS/56th FG

In reply to your letter requesting some information on aerial combat based on my experience, which I assure you is limited, I would like to make as short a reply as possible. In fact, I would much rather fight a battle than tell about it. However, I will be only too glad to give the points I consider foremost if they can be of the least amount of assistance to anyone else. I hope you can use them.

In my opinion, aerial combat isn't half of what it is shown to be in the movies. Most of us have some sort of an idea formed in our heads when we finally get into a combat theatre. We like to think that the battle will assume proportions equal to those of the movies. You know how it is – one pilot sees the other, they both grit their teeth to beat hell, and finally the deadly combat begins with violent manoeuvring by both parties. This field of thought is entirely erroneous. The combat usually takes place at a hell of a speed – the enemy aeroplane is only seen for a few seconds.

In nine cases out of ten the victor never sees his victim crash. As a result of the wrong idea, the new pilot who first sees a Jerry ship goes in to attack hell bent for election, and winds up feeling futile as the dickens because he didn't even succeed in frightening the Hun. I know, because I've done it myself many times. In fact, I've blown some darned good chances by just that sort of an attack.

The conclusion I draw from this is that no combat is worthwhile unless the attacking pilot does his work in a very cool and calculating way. I don't do it that way myself, but I think that if I have got things pretty well figured out before I make a bounce, I stand a much better chance of bagging that guy I'm going down after.

The cardinal points in an attack are first, be sure of your own position. See that there are no Jerries around to make an attack on you. Secondly, make sure that you know what the Hun is doing. Try to figure out what you would do if you were in his position. And thirdly, try to get up-sun on him. This is extremely important, because once the element of surprise is lost, the Jerry is about ten times as difficult to bring down.

Even if he is not surprised, he still can't see into the sun – so the chances of getting to him before he can make a turn are pretty darned good. last, close right up his old rudder and let go. Then he'll be a dead Hun. Now, there are what I consider to be the most important points of combat. Even though I don't practice them myself, at least I try to.

Before I ever saw a Jerry, I used to spend hours just sitting in the old sack thinking up just exactly what I would do if the Jerry was in such and such a position, and what I would do if he was doing something else. I think that it all paid off in the long run. A couple of times I have been fortunate in running into just the situation I had dreamed of at one time or another. Then, I didn't have to think. I just acted, because I had mentally been in that very position before. I believe it helped. At least I would advocate it. I still do it, and I hope that I run into a couple more of the dream castles, because it pays big dividends.

Yet another great USAAF official photograph featuring 56th FG aces. 1st Robert Johnson (left) shakes hands with Cap Walker M 'Bud' Mahurin while the crew chief adds victory number 14 to the latter's P-47D-5 42-8487 *"SPIRIT OF ATLANTIC CITY, N.J."*. This photograph was taken soon after the historic bomber escort mission of 30 January 1944, which had seen the 56th FG become the first group to achieve 200 kills in the ETO. Its pilots had scored 14 victories without loss on this day, Mahurin downing a Ju 88 and claiming a second as a probable. Fellow ace Bob Johnson went one better, destroying both a Bf 109G and an 'Me 210' (actually an Me 410), boosting his tally to 14 kills too. This photograph was almost certainly staged, for Mahurin's P-47 is carrying a drop tank – its predecessor on 42-8487 would have been 'punched off' as soon as the ace encountered the enemy (*via Michael O'Leary*)

At the same time, I always imagine what I would do if I were making the attack. I have it all figured out, also, when the Hun is on my tail. It can happen any time, and sometimes has. I know that I don't consider the dreaming time wasted. It's a lot of fun, too.

In regard to looking behind and around, I realise that it is a subject that has been harped on by every guy that has ever spent one measly hour on a combat operation. It is an absolute necessity. The result is most obvious.

The Hun will never bag an American fighter if the Yank sees him coming in time to take proper evasive action. It is still a bad thing to spend all one's time looking behind.

The idea behind fighter aircraft is that they will seek out the enemy and destroy him. A pilot will never accomplish this aim by looking behind all of the time. He must divide all his time to where it will do him the most good. If he knows that there are Huns above him then for God's sake look in front and down. When you spot the Jerry, go down and get him. Everyone knows about this subject, so I think that I've said enough.

One thing that I believe should be stressed by all means is the reading of the mission reports of every group. Those daily summary reports that we get the next day after each mission are the most important of all the printed matter in our intelligence office. Both the bomber and fighter reports are good, because it is easy to see just what tactics the enemy has used against us. Also, it is easy to note just what changes have been made in previous days. I usually use this stuff to formulate some plan of attack that I would use if I were the German controller. Sometimes it works.

I know that I got my first victory from reading the mission reports turned in by Gene Roberts. On the day he first got a couple of Jerries, he put in the mission reports how the Jerry was lining up far out to the side and making head-on attacks on the bomber formation. Gene just happened to mention exactly how far away from the bombers the Jerries were.

On 17 August I went out to the spot where Gene found his and I got two of them out there (Editor's Note – two Fw 190 confirmed destroyed on the afternoon of 17 August 1943). Now, I'm a firm believer in the reports. So, I advocate that all pilots read them. I kind of wish that the accounts of the engagements were just a little more complete.

The next most important thing is the duty of all the positions in a squadron. I've been fortunate in that I have always been in a hitting position – leading a flight. I still think that it is the wingman who counts. I couldn't shoot down a thing if I were worrying about whether or not I had a wingman. He is the most important guy in the squadron.

It is up to the wingman to cover his element leader no matter what. Sure, I know it's tough to sit back and tell a guy that he is clear behind so he can shoot down a Jerry. But look at it this way. Sooner or later the guy you're following around is going to be through with his tour. That'll leave a vacancy. The guy who will fill it will be the guy who has been giving the perfect job as a wingman. He will then get the chance to shoot, and probably will have profited by following a good shot around. Then, too, he will realise just what an important job the wingman has.

A good wingman is worth his weight in API (Editor's Note – Armour-Piercing Incendiaries). So, for the wingmen, stick close to the man you fly with. Watch behind and let him look out in front. Fly well, and you will get to do all the shooting you want soon enough. I know I don't have to say a word about the leaders, because I've tried to beat all of them out of an attack from time to time, and it's almost impossible to get through the maze of Thunderbolts who have beaten me to the draw.

The last thing that I can stress is training. I think that my group probably does more training than any other in the ETO. At least, it seems that way to me. I've been training ever since I got to the group, and I imagine I'll continue to do so 'till the war is over. It really pays. Every worthwhile hour in the air is the most valuable thing that I know of. After all, we are fighting for our lives.

What's more, we are fighting for the most valuable thing in the world – Freedom. I think that these two things are well worth a little practice.

Aerial camera gunnery is absolutely the most valuable training a man can get. Almost exactly like the real thing, only played with our own ships. Next in importance comes formation – both tactical and close. A good formation flyer will almost manufacture gasoline – something of which we don't have enough as it is. Third comes acrobatics, because a guy who knows what his aeroplane will do won't have to worry about how to make it do it when he could use the time shooting down a Hun. Fourth, anyone knows just how good a red-hot outfit looks when they take off and land. They really look good.

This is all done by practice, and don't think they don't feel proud of themselves when they do make good landings and take-offs. I know, because I'm in one of those red-hot outfits, and it makes me feel good as hell. The same old axiom applies, 'Anything worth doing is worth doing well'.

Besides aerial camera work, I don't know of a thing that closely parallels shooting in combat. I certainly wish I did. My shooting is probably the worst in the whole Air Force. I know that most of us feel the same. Jerry Johnson is probably the best shot in the Air Force, but he won't tell me how he does it. I have to get close enough to the Hun to reach out and club him before I can hit him. Usually, even that won't work. But, boy if I knew how to practice shooting, I would spend all my waking hours at it.

If we, and I speak of the Air Forces as a whole, could only shoot perfectly, we would double our score with no effort at all. When the man does come forth who has invented a way of simulating combat, complete with shooting down the target, then we will win the air war hands down.

Well Sir, I think that I've said enough. I only hope that someone can get one iota of sense from this letter. If someone does, I will know that the time has been well spent. Thanks for asking me what I think – you gave me a chance to blow off a bit.

## Walker Melville 'Bud' Mahurin

Mahurin was born in Ann Arbor, Michigan, on 5 December 1918. He went on to join the Army Reserves on 29 September 1941, where he entered flight training. Commissioned as a pilot on 29 April 1942 at Ellington Field, Texas, Mahurin was then assigned to the 63rd FS/56th FG at Boxted in England. On 17 August the 56th flew as escort for Eighth Air Force bombers heading to Schweinfurt and Regensburg. Encountering a heavy force of enemy fighters, Mahurin shot down two Fw 190s. He went on to became an ace on 4 October, and had achieved ten kills by the end of November. On 21 March 1944 he was promoted to major, and shared a victory over a Do 217 six days later. However, Mahurin's Thunderbolt was hit by return fire from the bomber and set ablaze during this engagement, forcing him to bail out. With the help of the French underground, the ace evaded the Germans and returned to England.

Due to the AAF ruling which prevented escaping aircrew from returning to their original unit, Mahurin was transferred to the South-west Pacific as commanding officer of the 3rd Air Commando Squadron. Flying P-51Ds, and seeing combat from New Guinea to Okinawa, he became one of the few American aces to score kills against both the Germans and the Japanese when he added a Ki-46 'Dinah' to his tally on 14 January 1945. Mahurin returned to the United States soon afterwards, where he was promoted to lieutenant-colonel.

Staying in the Air Force after the war, Mahurin served two tours of duty in the Pentagon and went on to obtain an aeronautical engineering degree. During the Korean War he was assigned to the 25th Fighter Interceptor Group (FIG) and shot down 3.5 MiG-15s while flying F-86 Sabres. He was then transferred as commanding officer to the 4th FIG, but on 13 May 1952 his Sabre was shot down by ground fire. He subsequently spent 16 months as a PoW, undergoing extensive torture. At the end of the Korean War Mahurin returned to the USA and stayed in the USAF until 1956, when he entered the aerospace industry. He was credited with 20.75 victories in World War 2 (and 3.5 confirmed in Korea), along with three probables and one damaged.

'Bud' Mahurin enjoyed considerable good fortune during World War 2, for he successfully bailed out of three P-47s and crash-landed a fourth one (*via I J Phillips*)

## Capt Robert S Johnson
## 62nd FS/56th FG

A lot of green pilots fly good combat formation for the first, second or third mission. If they see no enemy, many of them get cocky and think combat is a cinch. They relax and maybe get away with it on several trips over enemy territory – then it happens. The first enemy they see or have contact with knocks them down simply because they saw him too late, or not at all. They were too relaxed to kick the aeroplane's rudder or roll the ship up on a wing and look behind and above them, as well as straight ahead or at their leaders.

It's much easier and better to come home tired with a sore neck from looking constantly in every direction and from constantly skidding sideways to look behind and around you than it is to leave the thing you sit on over enemy territory. Once in a while it's good business to put a wing tip up just over the sun and look around it, too. Often there is plenty of company there.

Never let a Jerry get his sights on you. No matter whether he is at 100 yards or at 1000 yards away, 20 mm will carry easily that far and will easily knock down an aeroplane at 1000 yards. It is better to stay at 20,000 ft with a good speed with a Jerry at 25,000 ft, than it is to pull up in his vicinity at a stalling speed. If he comes down on you pull up into him, and nine times out of ten, if you are nearly head-on with him he will roll away to his right. Then you have him. Roll on to his

Flying a total of 91 missions with the 56th FG, Robert S Johnson scored 28 victories before finishing his tour of duty and being sent home in early June 1944. During July and August of that same year, Dick Bong, flying a P-38, and Johnson, flying a P-47, toured the United States on a War Bond drive. Johnson commanded a US-based P-47 operational training unit until the end of the war. This photograph was taken soon after Johnson had increased his score to 26 kills (although only 25 swastikas are shown) on 13 April 1944 (*via Michael O'Leary*)

tail and go get him. If he tries to turn with you and can out-turn you, pull the nose up straight ahead and kick rudder and stick toward him and you can slice to the inside of him. The enemy thinks then that you are turning inside him and he will try to dive away from you – and your bullets!

Try this, and any other trick you can think of, in friendly combat.

Any time you lose your wingman or leader, you've lost 75 per cent of your eyes and fighting strength. Jerries will shoot at anyone. Never think you're a favourite to them. Anyone can get it – some of the best have gotten it. So keep your eyes open.

Battle-weary P-47D-11 42-75599 *MAXIMUM GOOSE/ Barbara Ann IV* was assigned to the 62nd FS's Lt W P Gordon in early 1944 (*via S Sox*)

P-47D-10 42-75125 *HAWKEYE* was also assigned to the 56th FG's 62nd FS. Note how it has been polished by its groundcrew – most P-47s in the ETO looked more like the aircraft seen above. All this hard work was done in an effort to eek out a few more miles per hour

## Robert Samuel Johnson

Born on 21 February 1920 in Lawton, Oklahoma, Johnson graduated from Cameron Junior College and went on to enter the aviation cadet programme in Class 42-F on 11 November 1941. Commissioned as a pilot on 3 July 1942 at Kelly Field, he was then transferred to the 56th FG's 61st FS, which was equipped with Thunderbolts at Stratford, Connecticut, on 20 July 1942. He sailed for England with the group on 13 January 1943.

Flying from Boxted, Johnson completed his first operational mission during April 1943 and scored his first victory, over an Fw 190, on 13 June. From that point on he began to rapidly compile an impressive victory list, becoming an ace on 10 October and a double ace on 31 December. Flying with the 62nd FS, Johnson scored his 27th victory on 8 May 1944 and was transferred back to America, where he teamed up with Pacific P-38 ace Richard Bong on a bond tour. He then took command of a Thunderbolt operational training unit in Abilene, Texas, for the rest of the war. Joining Republic Aviation after the end of the war, Johnson remained in the reserves and rose to the rank of lieutenant-colonel. He passed away in 1999. With a final tally of 27 confirmed and three damaged, he was the second highest scoring American ace in the ETO.

Bob Johnson's career in the front-line came to an abrupt end soon after he became the first pilot in the ETO to better the score of ranking American World War 1 ace, Eddie Rickenbacker. Deemed too valuable to lose in combat by senior USAAF officers, Johnson was transferred out of the 56th FG after scoring his 27th and 28th kills on 8 May 1944 (*via Tom Ivie*)

## LT COL HARRY J DAYHUFF 78th FG

Always turn into the attack if you see it coming. If the Hun is right on your tail do something quick and violent. As one of our pilots once said when the first he was aware of a Hun were the tracers going by his shoulder, 'I put the stick in one corner and the rudder in the other. I don't know what happened, but when I came out the Hun wasn't there any longer'.

If there is a cloud handy, use it, but change your course once inside.

If outnumbered, dive like hell – that is in a Thunderbolt – other fighter types may prefer other methods.

If attacked while on the deck you are in a bad spot, and you can either turn into the attack or try and outrun them. If the Hun is in shooting range, always keep the ball going in each corner – never give him an opportunity to line up his sights. Remember this slows you up though.

Most successful offensive action comes with superior speed and altitude coupled with surprise. Always use the sun or blind spots to obtain surprise.

Watch for overhauling the victim too rapidly, and although you probably won't on your fist kill, try to avoid opening fire until you are in good shooting range.

The enemy will usually split-S, but you can follow him in a P-47 if you haven't already got him. At the present time it appears okay to stay with him until he is definitely destroyed.

Volumes could be written about a good wingman, and too often they are the unsung heroes of combat. They make it possible for the leaders to get victories. In offensive action a wingman is responsible for

**Formerly CO of the 78th FG's 82nd FS, Lt Col Harry Dayhuff was assigned to the 352nd FG during its 'breaking in' period in the ETO. A highly experienced P-47 pilot, he led the 352nd on its first three missions, in September 1943 (*via Garry L Fry*)**

Photographed at Duxford soon after being declared operational, pilots from the 78th FG's 84th FS pose in front of P-47C-5 41-6630 *Spokane Chief*. This aircraft was the mount of the unit's CO, Maj Eugene P Roberts, who can be seen sat on the grass, third from the left, in the very front row. To the CO's left is the 78th FG's future ranking ace, Quince L Brown (12.333 kills), whilst behind Roberts is Peter E Pompetti (five kills). Finally, to Pompetti's left is future 84th FS CO, and five-kill ace, Jack C Price (*via Aeroplane*)

**Left**
Capt Charles Pershing London of Oklahoma City became VIII Fighter Command's first ace when he claimed an Fw 190 and a Bf 109 over Haltern, in north-western Germany, on 30 July 1943. These successes took his score to exactly five kills. London subsequently failed to add any further victories to his tally during the remainder of his tour with the 78th FG's 83rd FS, which came to an end on 1 November 1943. All of his kills were claimed in his distinctively marked P-47C-5 41-6335 *EL JEEPO*. This particular photograph of the ace and his aircraft was taken prior to London scoring his first kill on 14 May 1943 (*via Bill Hess*)

keeping the leader's tail covered, as the leader's whole attention is devoted to the enemy in front.

Unless hopelessly outnumbered, these days I would consider it advisable to attack always, as the average Hun doesn't like to scrap with us. There are, of course, obvious exceptions to this.

There is little use in trying great deflection shots (above 30 degrees) unless it is the only shot you get. Keep the ball in the middle.

Normally, I would break off combat with a sharp climbing turn in case an enemy is trying to bounce you.

Formations should be defensive as well as offensive, which means flying with good cross-cover – flights and ships so placed as to watch each other's tail.

All outfits in this theatre are using the basic four-ship flight, but outfits vary as to formation used while with bombers. Some form of weaving is necessary, no matter what type of support is given, to stay with the slower bombers. The whole outfit may weave or individual flights may weave.

All outfits I am acquainted with allow four-ship flights freedom of independent action once enemy aircraft are sighted.

If they have ample warning, group or squadron leaders will designate who is to make the bounce, or may take it themselves. But generally there is insufficient time for this, and flights will have already started on a bounce by the time they are calling it.

Our flights fly abreast as much as possible if the flight is not weaving with the ships stacked in pretty close.

On flying to and from a rendezvous with bombers, I prefer the group to be flown as compactly as possible, still maintaining cross-cover. This enables leaders to know which ships are his, and any other ships sighted would be recorded as enemy. New outfits often have the right idea, but

once up at altitude they tend to keep spreading out until they are continually reporting their own ships as 'bandits' or 'bogies'.

I am purposely saying little about actual methods or protecting bombers because of the many methods used, and the many factors which affect the practice used such as the number of bombers to protect, the bomber formation being spread out, the bombers being late, etc. This usually puts the load on the shoulders of the group leader, and it is up to him to decide how to use his force to take care of the situation at hand. If a formation is attacked, all ships in the formation should turn into the attack.

As stated previously, who makes a bounce is determined in actual practice by who sees the enemy first and who is the closest. One occasion which might arise in exception to this would be of a whole group going into a bomber rendezvous, sighting one or two lone enemy aircraft some distance off. Then, the group leader would designate someone in the formation to attack without disrupting the group formation.

We adopt the general rule of having one flight (of four) go down on a bounce, with another following it for top cover.

If the enemy has the advantage of altitude and position, there is little you can do except keep your eye on him or, if keeping him away from the bombers, you could climb toward him to scare him off.

# MAJ DON BODENHAMER JR 78th FG

## Individual Combat Tactics

### DEFENSIVE

Always break violently into the attack. Never break level. Break either up or slightly down – preferably the latter, as this makes it difficult for the Hun to pull deflection. Keep your altitude, and keep your eyes on the Hun. Hit the deck only as the last resort.

If a Hun latches himself firmly onto your tail and you can't out-turn him, hit the deck, barrel-rolling vertically. Have your gyro compass uncaged, straighten out on home course and *fly straight*. Use cloud cover if available.

By the time this photograph was taken at Duxford in late August 1943, Gene Roberts had claimed six of his eventual nine kills. A close examination of this shot reveals seven swastikas below the cockpit of the *Spokane Chief*, which suggests that the CO of the 84th FS was convinced in his own mind that the Fw 190 he claimed as a probable on 1 July 1943 had actually crashed. By 20 October Roberts had run his score to nine kills, six of which he downed with this very aircraft. Promoted to lieutenant colonel and made Deputy CO of the 78th FG in late September 1943, he was declared tour-expired after completing his 89th combat mission with the group some three months later. Lt Col Roberts returned to the frontline with the Eighth Air Force in January 1945 when he assumed command of the P-51D-equipped 364th FG at Honington. Despite leading the group through to the end of the war, he failed to add any kills to his tally of nine destroyed with the 78th FG (*via Bill Hess*)

The Hun nearly always dives to the deck after a bounce. By following him down and staying slightly underneath, you can catch him with his head up on the deck where he can't get away.

Always attack out of the sun if possible, and break back up into it. Don't forget to keep an eye on it yourself! Use cloud cover when in trouble. If there is a solid low overcast you can fly just on top to prevent attacks from below – then you can pop right in if bounced from above. Don't fly over the top of a thin overcast!

When caught by superior numbers of enemy aircraft above, I endeavour to get directly beneath them – before the bounce. It is very difficult, if not impossible, to bounce anyone directly beneath you. If caught on the deck with the Hun behind you, all you can do is fly straight, run like hell, and use the terrain for cover. If they are parallel, break into, and over the top of them – force them into the ground. It has been my experience that the Hun gets a little panicky when faced with violent manoeuvres at a low altitude.

Wingmen should break into an attack, doing everything possible to disrupt it, including shooting the Hun off me. I would endeavour to bring the Hun into a good position so the wingman could polish him off.

I would hit the deck only when I couldn't get the Hun off my tail by any other method.

### OFFENSIVE

I attack out of the sun, coming up slightly underneath, with my wingman in trail and slightly to one side, watching our tails. I attempt to close as rapidly as possible to about 600-800 yards, then I chop throttle and close slowly – I find this prevents overshooting. I break away as violently as possible into the sun, meanwhile clearing my tail. I attempt to stay dead astern until I shoot him down – once there, stick until you get him! Many a Hun has been lost because he wasn't followed down.

I have never had a Jerry break into me. They always hit the deck. Follow them.

When attacking superior numbers, hit the highest, or the farthest back – and naturally, any stragglers. Zoom back up and repeat until they are completely broken up, then go to work on the pieces.

Learn deflection and *range*, and use them! The best way to shoot a Jerry is dead astern, opening up at 300 yards. Incidentally, this is pretty hard to do on your first few Jerries. Indeed, experience is the only cure.

**Although not an ace, Maj Don Bodenhammer Jr nevertheless made a major contribution to the success of the 78th FG in the bomber escort role during the group's first year in the ETO (*via Garry L Fry*)**

# Formation Combat Tactics

## GENERAL

Our climb formation is as follows – individual aeroplanes in close formation, flights line abreast, sections line astern, with the last section above the first two. Squadrons fly line astern. The main purpose is to keep a compact group formation, and maintain cross-cover.

After the bombers are reached, each squadron takes a box and covers. Each section in the squadron takes a certain area and covers.

Flights stay together at all times, and sections stay together until contact with enemy aircraft is made. Flights are free to bounce, and elements within the flight can bounce if the flight leader is given a call so he can cover.

Flights in sections fly in supporting distance of each other, close enough so that a good cross-cover is maintained.

After combat it is impossible to reform a squadron. We generally have a designated spot where we attempt to gather our forces, say at nine o'clock on the first box of bombers and 2000 ft above.

The more area you cover the greater the chance for combat. Eight-aeroplane sections should be free to roam about as they please. They make a hard-hitting offensive unit, and are strong defensively.

## DEFENSIVE

When enemy aircraft are in a position to bounce, I constantly change position, manoeuvring to prevent them from positioning themselves.

The larger the enemy formation, the easier it is to mix them up. Break up their co-ordination and you are boss.

I drop belly tanks only if actually bounced, as you can get rid of them damn fast when necessary. If they are nearly empty they don't affect the manoeuvrability of the aircraft.

The Hun still uses 'decoys', usually a lone 'sitter', or perhaps twin-engined stuff.

After combat I gather the formation by 360 degree turns, enabling my flight to cut me off and regain formation.

I always brief my flight on what I will probably do, and what is expected of them. I make sure they know the courses in and out, as well as the timings, the task force we have and what enemy reaction to expect.

I would order a formation to hit the deck only as a last resort.

## OFFENSIVE

Flights are free to bounce at any time. Elements may bounce with permission of the flight leader who covers. The decision I make as to

Still very much a lowly flight officer when this photograph was taken 'for the folks back home' in Woodbine, New Jersey, Peter Pompetti would go on to become one of only four aces created by the 84th FS in the ETO. He is sat on his P-47C-5 41-6393 *"Axe the Axis"*, which he flew from July 1943 through to January 1944. The solitary swastika below the fighter's cockpit records his first combat victory (a Bf 109), claimed on 30 July over Holland. Pompetti scored a further three kills (and three damaged) with this aircraft prior to it being replaced by a P-47D-6 in February 1944. Achieving ace status on 4 January 1944, he was shot down by flak whilst strafing near Paris on 17 March and made a PoW. By then a veteran first lieutenant, Peter Pompetti was flying his 95th combat mission at the time (*via Bill Hess*)

Ranking 78th FG ace Quince Brown poses with his dog on the wing of his assigned fighter, P-47D-6 42-74753 *OKIE*. A native of Hydrok, Oklahoma (hence the aircraft's nickname), Brown claimed 7.333 of his 12.333 kills with this Thunderbolt, which he flew from September 1943 through to March 1944. Note the white broom markers behind his head, which denoted successful combat 'sweeps' made by the 84th FS over Occupied Europe. Promoted to major, and serving as the 84th FS's Operations Officer, Brown was less than two weeks into his second tour with the 78th FG when his P-47D was downed by flak whilst strafing Vogelsand airfield, in Germany, on 8 September 1944. He successfully bailed out of his stricken fighter and was quickly captured upon landing in enemy territory. However, rather than being sent off to a PoW camp, Brown was murdered by a *Schutzstaffel* (SS) officer later that same day (*via Bill Hess*)

This graphic gun camera footage was more than enough to secure a 78th FG P-47 pilot a confirmed kill over a Bf 109G in early 1944 (*via John Stanaway*)

whether elements should bounce depends on the experience of the element leader.

Send down the maximum number to take care of the enemy aircraft. However, it is advisable not to send too many, as they only get in each others' way. Never send more than one for one.

If the enemy has a superior position, attempt to lure him out of it and take over yourself. Make him commit himself – once that is done he must carry through.

Three months ago it would have been bad tactics to pursue the Hun away from the bombers, but now we are to knock out the Luftwaffe, so

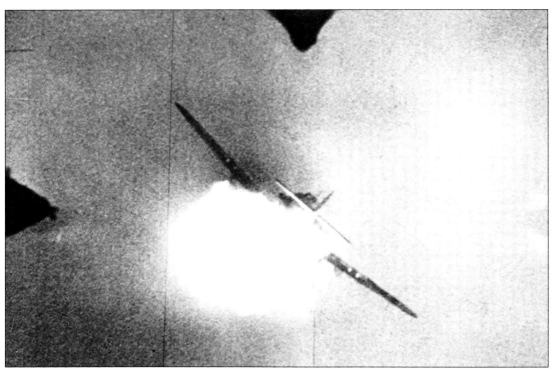

I say 'Stick with them 'til you get them!' Coupled with this is the fact that generally the eight-aeroplane section is the only one in the flight, so that still leaves adequate cover with the bombers. Jerries are getting too scarce to let them get away! If you are on deep penetration with only a few friendly fighters and lots of Huns, I would advise staying with the bombers.

Always attack before they can reach the bombers. You aren't doing the bombers any good after they are shot down. Besides, Jerry is so busy watching the bombers that you can blow him up before he knows you are there.

You can use the sun to some extent as a screen, but clouds, in my opinion, are more of a hindrance than a help. If you hide, you are generally in a bad position to help the bombers when they need it. If high in the sun, they attack from below, and if low they attack from above. The best thing to do is split up the squadron into sections. These smaller numbers are harder to see, and they can mingle with the bombers and act like Jerries.

Be aggressive, seek out the Hun and destroy him. Keep him on the defensive. Have a flexible, defensively sound formation, and use teamwork in place of numbers.

(OFFICIAL NOTE – Maj Bodenhamer says the enemy, under attack, always hits the deck. 'Always' is too strong a word, and there are many, many instances when the Hun has turned into the attack instead. The better he is, the more apt he is to do so.)

## COL JOE L MASON
## COMMANDING OFFICER
## 352nd FG

We operate a basic formation of an eight-ship section – two flights, with one flight covering the other at all times.

I firmly believe that this eight-ship section can fight any number of Huns at any altitude at any place – *provided* that it flies it correctly – each man doing his part.

It is impossible for a formation to get bounced before it's too late to do anything about it if everyone is doing his job. This is based on the theory of cross-cover – line abreast or nearly so. The same principle holds good whether it's a two-ship formation or a 200-ship formation.

He who hesitates is lost. This goes if it's a bounce or if you are the one that is bounced. I would at this point have killed more Germans if I had not hesitated so long on my bounces.

The more Huns you see the easier the next one will be. And the same goes for the kills, each one gets easier than the last.

The wingmen who don't lose their leaders regardless of what they do are the wingmen who win the battle, and the war. When attacked by superior forces, a good offence is the best defence, *and* the best bluff. Other than that just fight like hell.

Stay off the deck unless you have business there. Why let everyone and his brother take a shot at you! If the fight goes that low – then

Inspirational leader of the 352nd FG, Col Joe 'Big Red' Mason flew P-47D-5 42-8466 from the autumn of 1943 through to the spring of 1944. This aircraft was personalised with the badge of the 59th FS (with whom Mason had previously served) and the name *"GENA THIS IS IT"*. The latter slogan was added some while after the 'Roaring Lion' artwork, and came about when Mason wrote to his wife telling her that he had named his P-47 after her. She in turn asked for a photo of the said fighter, and the colonel hastily had her name added to his Thunderbolt!
(*352nd FG Association*)

good cross-cover with your wingman and flight will bring you back upstairs where you can fight some more.

Break off the attack when the German is dead, or the question arises as to whether you and your flight can get home or not.

Faith in yourself and your ability to kill a German will give you the determination to press your attack to a successful conclusion.

The bomber support itself depends on how many fighters you have to cover a certain number of bombers. The greater the fighter depth the better the support. Depth in this case meaning the amount of sky in all directions from the bombers that you can saturate with fighters.

You must look at the situation upon rendezvous and place your forces accordingly where they will do the most good. The group leader must know at all times where all parts of his group are.

Use the bomber formation as a reference point in putting your group back together after combat or escort. If the ground can be seen,

Joe Mason scored just one of his five kills in a Thunderbolt, downing a Bf 109 over Germany in *"GENA THIS IS IT"* on 24 February 1944. His remaining victories were claimed in P-51B-10 42-106609 on 8 and 13 May 1944 (*352nd FG Association*)

then that can be used too. On pulling out, enough strength should be put together to offer mutual support. The Hun will hesitate to bounce a unit which looks like it knows what is going on, and has sufficient numbers to repel an attack.

I do not think the Hun has changed his tactics of not fighting unless he has superior advantages, and numbers.

---

### Joe Lennard Mason

Born in Washington, DC, on 10 April 1915, Joe Mason went on to attend college for three years, during which time he obtained a private pilot's license and flew 500 hours, before joining the Army on 10 October 1937. Entering the aviation cadet programme, he graduated on 5 October 1938 from Kelly Field. An experienced pilot by the time the USA entered World War 2, Mason rapidly rose in rank, going from first lieutenant in 1941 to lieutenant colonel on 3 March 1943. He became CO of the 352nd FG, which was working up on Thunderbolts at Republic Field, in New York, during May 1943.

Taking the group overseas, Mason arrived at Bodney on 7 July 1943 and the 352nd commenced combat operations during September. Promoted to full colonel on 20 November, Mason scored his first victory on 24 February 1944 when he shot down a Bf 109 near Schwagstorf, in Germany.

During April 1944 the group converted to the Mustang and began flying long-range escort missions for bombers of the Eighth Air Force. On 8 May, it successfully defended the bombers against a numerically superior Luftwaffe attack near Brunswick, claiming 19 fighters destroyed. For this action, the 352nd was awarded a Distinguished Unit Citation. During the battle Mason shot down an Fw 190 and damaged another. Just five days later, while on an escort mission to the same area, he became an ace after downing two Bf 109s and an Fw 190 – he also damaged a third Messerschmitt.

Staying in the air force post-war, Mason commanded the 49th FG during the Korean War. He retired from the USAF in 1967 and died of cancer on 16 June 1974.

Mason's final tally was five destroyed and two damaged.

---

# LT COL JOHN C MEYER
# COMMANDING OFFICER
# 352nd FG

In every case when attacked by enemy aircraft I have turned into the attack. We have found that the turning characteristics of the P-47 as against the Me 109 and Fw 190 are very nearly equal. Since when we are attacked the enemy aircraft has almost always come from above, he has excessive speed, and turning inside him is a simple matter. If the enemy aircraft is sighted in time, it is often possible to turn into him

**Boasting individual canvas canopy and engine covers to keep out the all-pervading winter dampness, P-47Ds of the 352nd FG's 487th FS await the arrival of the squadron's groundcrews at Bodney in late 1943 (*via Sam Sox*)**

for a frontal attack. On two occasions I was able to do this, and the enemy aircraft was reluctant to trade a head-on pass and broke for the deck. Thus I was able to turn a defensive situation into an offensive one.

The sun is a most effective offensive weapon and the Hun loves to use it. Whenever possible I always try to make all turns into the sun and try never to fly with it at my back. Clouds are very effective for evasive action if there is eight-tenths' coverage or better. They're a good way to get home when you're alone.

When attacked by far superior numbers, I get the hell out of there using speed, or clouds (there are usually plenty around in this theatre), and only as a last resort by diving to the deck. An aggressive act in the initial phases of the attack will very often give you a breather and a head start home.

I had one experience which supports this last statement, and also shows what teamwork can do. My wingman and I, attacking a pair of '109s, were in turn attacked by superior numbers of enemy aircraft. In spite of this (the enemy aircraft attacking us were still out of range for effective shooting) we continued our attack, each of us destroying one of the enemy aircraft, and then turned into our attackers. Our attackers broke off and regained the tactical advantage of altitude, but during this brief interval we were able to effect our escape in the clouds. Showing a willingness to fight often discourages the Hun even when he outnumbers us, while on the other hand I have, by immediately breaking for the deck on other occasions, given the Hun a 'shot in the arm', turning his half-hearted attack into an aggressive one.

I do not like the deck. This is especially true in the Pas de Calais area. I believe that it may be used effectively to avoid an area of numerically superior enemy aircraft because of the difficulty in seeing an aircraft on the deck from above. With-all silver aeroplanes, this excuse is even doubtful. The danger from small arms ground fire, especially near the coast, is great. I realise that I differ from some of my contemporaries in this respect, but two-thirds of our squadron losses have been from enemy small arms fire.

Just recently I led a 12-ship squadron on a 50-mile penetration of the Pas de Calais area on the deck. We were under fire along the entire route. We lost one pilot, three aeroplanes, and three others damaged. I repeat, I don't like the deck, and can see little advantage in being there. Caught on the deck by three '190s, I was able to lose them by using water injection.

Mainly it's my wingman's eyes that I want. One man cannot see enough. When attacked, I want first for him to warn me, then for him to think. Every situation is different, and the wingman must have initiative and ability to size up the situation properly and act accordingly. There is no rule of thumb for a wingman.

I attempt to attack out of the sun. If the enemy aircraft is surprised, he's duck soup, but time is an important factor and it should not be wasted in securing position. I like to attack quickly and at high speed. This gives the enemy aircraft less time to see you and less time to act. Also, speed can be converted to altitude on the break away. The wingman's primary duty is protection of his element leader.

It takes the leader's entire attention to destroy an enemy aircraft. If he takes time to cover his own tail, he may find the enemy has 'flown the coop'. Effective gunnery takes maximum mental and physical concentration. The wingman flies directly in trail on the attack. This provides manoeuvrability, and he is there to follow up the attack if his leader misses. Once, however, the wingman has cleared himself and is certain his element is not under attack, he may move out and take one of the other enemy aircraft under attack if more than one target is available. Good wingmen, smart wingmen, are the answer to a leader's prayers.

If surprise is not effected the enemy aircraft generally turns into the attack and dives down, thus causing the attacker to overshoot. When this happens I like to break off the attack and resume the tactical advantage of altitude.

Often the enemy aircraft will pull out of his dive and attempt to climb back up. Then another attack can be made. A less experienced enemy pilot will often just break straight down. Then it is possible, and often fairly easy, to follow him. Usually on the way down he will kick, skid and roll his aircraft in violent evasive action for

Virtually all VIII Fighter Command aircraft carried nicknames or nose-art, some of which were quite risqué. An example of the latter was *MissBehave*, whose svelte female form graced the cowling of Lt Robert Berkshire's P-47D-2 42-22515 in the autumn of 1943. This artwork was considered to be too provocative by Berkshire's CO, Maj John Meyer, and it was replaced by a chain mace wielding Amazonian woman with arms as thick as tree trunks! (*352nd FG Association*)

which the only answer is point blank range. Compressibility is a problem which must be taken into consideration when following an enemy aircraft in a dive.

The effect of superior numbers in a decision to attack is small. The tactical advantage of position, altitude, sun and direction of attack are the influencing factors. With these factors in my favour the number of enemy aircraft are irrelevant.

It is not wise to attack when the enemy has the advantage of altitude, and as long as he maintains it. If you're closing fast enough to overshoot, you're closing fast enough to get point blank range. At point blank range you can't miss.

I am not a good shot. Few of us are. To make up for this I hold my fire until I have a shot of less than 20 degrees deflection and until I'm within 300 yards. Good discipline on this score can make up for a great deal.

I like to attack at high speeds and break up into the sun, making the break hard just in case his friend is around. Then I like to get back that precious altitude.

En route to rendezvous we fly a formation which has for its basis mutual protection rather than flexibility or manoeuvrability. The group is broken down into three squadrons of 16 ships each. The squadrons are stepped up, with the second squadron about 1000 ft higher, into the sun and line abreast, and the third squadron 2500 ft higher than the lead squadron on the down sun side and line abreast. This alignment makes it impossible for any one squadron to be bounced out of the sun by an attacker who is not clear of the sun to one of the other squadrons. The flights fly in line abreast, providing mutual cross cover between individual aeroplanes and flights within the squadron.

Upon rendezvousing with the bombers, the group generally breaks down into eight-ship sections of two flights, each operating independently and at various ranges from the main bomber force. One flight of this section remains in close support of the other on bounces. This method has been the most successful one tried by this organisation. It has certain disadvantages in that they may run into superior forces, in which case considerably more would have been achieved by keeping a larger portion of our force intact.

However, our main problem to date has been in seeking out the enemy, rather than his destruction once found. This method of deployment has been the best answer to that problem. These eight ships are under orders to remain within supporting distance of each other at all times. These sections operate above, below, around, ahead, behind and well out to the sides of the main bomber force. The extent of ranging is dependent upon many factors such as weather, number of friendly fighters in the vicinity and what information we may have as to enemy disposition – the decision on this is left up to the section leaders.

There is no rule of thumb limitation on who makes bounces. The primary job of the flight leaders is that of seeking out bounces, while that of the other members of the flight is flight protection. If any member of a flight sees a bounce and time permits, he notifies his flight leader and the flight leader leads the engagement. However, if the flight leader is unable to see the enemy, the one who spotted him takes over the lead, or in those cases (of which there are many) when the time element is precious, the man who sees the enemy acts immediately, calling in the bounce as he goes.

Usually if the combat is of any size or duration, flights become separated. The element of two becoming separated, however, is a cardinal and costly sin. We find it almost impossible for elements to rejoin their squadrons or flights after any prolonged combat. However, there are generally friendly fighters in the vicinity all with the same intention and we join any of them. A friendly fighter is a friend indeed, no matter what outfit he's from.

Recently we have tried imitating Hun formations, but have not had any particular success with it.

On the defensive, the eight-ship section turns into them, presenting a 64-gun array which the enemy is reluctant to face. If we are hopelessly outnumbered, or low on gas after the initial turn, the individual ships keep increasing their bank until in a vertical dive, using the superior diving speed of the P-47 for escape. On one occasion when we were extremely low on gas, one flight of our eight was bounced by three '190s. That flight broke for the deck with the '190s following. We crossed over, following the '190s down. They immediately broke off their attack and zoomed back up. We continued our dive and effected our escape.

We drop belly tanks when empty. Gas consumption is a primary tactical consideration in this theatre, and we don't like to use it to drag empty belly tanks around.

The number of aircraft to go down on a bounce is influenced purely by the number of enemy aircraft. In any case, at least one flight stays several thousand feet above until the situation is carefully sized up, at which time the leader of that flight makes the decision on whether to join the fray or stay aloft.

We pursue all attacks to conclusion, or whilst a favourable conclusion seems possible. In other words, if by continuing the pursuit it seems reasonable the enemy may be destroyed. There are exceptions to this, however. As for instance, the Hun sometimes will send a single aircraft across our nose to draw us away from the bombers while their main force attacks. This must be watched for, and the decision made by the flight leaders.

Every effort is made to hit the enemy while he is forming for the bomber attack. Generally, he forms ahead and well to the up sun side of the bomber force. A large part of our group force is deployed in that area.

Our group was the first to attempt a penetration in force on the deck for a strafing mission. Out of this experiment I have these recommendations to make: that penetration to within ten miles of the coast be made on the deck, then the force to zoom to 8000-12,000 ft, navigating at that altitude, penetrating beyond the target, then hitting the deck at some prominent point a short distance from the target and then proceeding to it. I firmly recommend this style of attack, rather than penetration all the way on the deck where the enemy small arms fire is intense and pinpoint navigation impossible. Finally, when an aircraft is below 8000 ft over enemy territory, it should be flown just as low as possible. Twenty feet above the ground is too high.

(Official note – The episode cited illustrating the value of the initial aggressiveness seems a dangerously fine estimate of the situation, only possible because the enemy was sighted well in advance. Otherwise, they might have been victims of a typical enemy sucker play.)

## John C Meyer

John Meyer was born on 3 April 1919 in Brooklyn, New York, and he subsequently attended Dartmouth College. He joined the Army Reserves and became a flying cadet, being commissioned a pilot and second lieutenant on 26 July 1940 at Kelly Field. His first assignment was as a flight instructor, and he remained in this posting for a year. Meyer was then transferred to the 33rd PS in Iceland to fly convoy patrols, before returning to the USA to join the 352nd FG in Massachusetts. He was made commanding officer of the group's 487th FS on 28 December 1942.

**Fourth-ranking air-to-air ace in the ETO, John 'Whips' Meyer actually topped VIII Fighter Command's overall ace listing at war's end due to the Eighth Air Force's unique way of according strafing victories the same significance as aerial successes. He claimed 24 aircraft shot down and 13 destroyed in strafing attacks. This photograph was taken at Bodney in May 1944, and it shows Lt Col Meyer sat in his P-51B-10 42-106471, his score then standing at 8.5 aerial kills (*352nd FG Association*)**

Meyer became a captain on 21 January 1943 and took the P-47-equipped 487th to Britain that June. The unit commenced combat operations in September, flying a series of bomber escort missions. On 26 November the now Maj Meyer scored his first victory when he downed a Bf 109. During April 1944 the unit began converting to the Mustang, and Meyer enjoyed his first success in the North American fighter on 10 April. On 8 May he celebrated his promotion to the rank of lieutenant colonel with a triple-kill haul that gave him ace status.

Meyer and the Mustang were a formidable duo, and he rapidly pushed his score past the 20-kill mark – this tally included two 'triples' and a 'double' haul. In February 1945 he was sent back to the USA, tour-expired.

Staying in the air force post-war, Meyer assumed command of the 4th FIG in August 1950, and led the Sabre-equipped unit to Korea, where he destroyed two MiG-15s. Meyer eventually rose to the rank of general, and Commander of Strategic Air Command. Retiring on 1 August 1974, he died of a heart attack while jogging on a Los Angeles beach on 2 December 1975. His final tally was 26 confirmed, one probable and three damaged.

# CAPT VIRGIL K MERONEY
# 487th FS/352nd FG

After reading your letter over several times, and giving it much thought, I have decided to write to you, in a sort of outline form, on several points I have learned while over here, and in combat against the enemy.

When we get replacements, they know practically nothing of the many things that go towards making a good fighter pilot. Their training, before we get them, is a headache in itself what with all the safety precautions and all that they have back in the States. So I won't go into that.

Here are some of my experiences.

## Individual Combat:

**A. Defensive** – on several occasions, I have been at a disadvantage when first seeing the enemy aircraft, but so far I have always been able to alter the situation by doing some quick thinking and acting. There is a lot of argument on whether the P-47 can out-turn the Fw 190 and the Me 109. I feel that it all depends on the situation of the moment. If you are bounced from above, you cannot out-dive them, since they had more speed than you to start with. Before you can gain any additional speed you're a dead pigeon!

Having learned that, I have always chopped my throttle and turned into them, turning in whatever direction I saw them coming from over my shoulder. I have always been able to out-turn them in that manner. After that, you can, according to the situation, either press home your attack or get the hell out! When attacked by vastly superior numbers of enemy aircraft, I have always found that by turning into them, and barrelling into them, they have always broken up their formation, and

P-47D-5 42-8460 *The Flying Scot!* was the mount of 486th FS pilot Lt Murdock Cunningham. Note the steam train depicted in artwork beneath the aircraft's nickname. Murdock can be seen strapping into the fighter at the start of yet another long-range escort mission in late 1943, the pilot being helped on with his seat straps by the aircraft's dedicated groundcrewmen, S/Sgt Vlator and Cpl Lincourt (*via Sam Sox*)

I've been able to single out one and get him! It helps a helluva lot if your wingman is right with you. If, unfortunately, your flight finds itself alone, it usually works out best if the elements split. Still, it is advisable that they keep each other in sight to offer mutual protection – that old teamwork again.

**B. Offensive** – when making an attack on an enemy aircraft, I like my wingman to stay back more than normal, so that he can stay with me more easily. If he stays abreast of me, his wing will very likely blank me out at times and he will lose me.

Usually, the enemy aircraft tries to hit the deck and kick the ship around while going down. It makes me very happy when they do that because then all I have to do is close up and let them have it! But I have noticed that the smart guys try to turn into you, and if you've come down from several thousand feet above them, you cannot stay with them. I have always found it works out best if you pull back up and do a sort of wing over. In that manner, you're bound to end up on their tail.

To keep from overshooting, I've always started throttling way back as soon as I get in range, and started firing. In that manner they are finished off before I overshoot them!

I think it is inadvisable to attack when you spot a single aeroplane far below you, even if the whole squadron is with you. If you do, you're bound to be on the deck before you finish him off, the whole squadron will be drawn away from their job with the bombers, and a lot of time and altitude will be wasted.

When I first did any shooting, like lots of other pilots, I opened up way out of range, and I'm convinced that range estimation cannot be emphasised too strongly.

**C. Group and Squadron Formation** – up until a few months ago, I was an element leader, so I don't think there is much I can say concerning group and squadron formations and tactics. However, these are some of the ways our squadron operates.

Each flight can make a bounce – the others will cover. We try to keep a section of two flights together at all times. In the flight, the element leader can make the attack while calling it in, and the flight leader and his wingman will follow him. Insofar as the wingmen are concerned, they can lead the attack only if the flight leader or element leader cannot see the enemy aircraft. They are the ones who will tell the wingman to go ahead, and that they will follow. If the wingman peels off and leaves his flight, he may get one or two enemy aircraft, but the chances are he'll never get back to get his name in *The Stars and Stripes* for it – the old Air Discipline.

Position for a bounce is good if you have it, but usually if you try to get it after seeing the enemy aircraft, he will get away. You have to go right after him the minute you see him!

Insofar as tactics are concerned, I think we should change them, and should experiment with different types of formations as much and as often as possible – if for no other reason than just to confuse the enemy. For example, send a group on penetration support, so that they rendezvous head-on with the bombers, and tail-on, when giving withdrawal support. It doesn't take the Germans long to find out any new rules.

That is it, for what it's worth. Now for that beer – I need it! I believe the main things are teamwork, confidence in your leaders, your ships, and that old fighting heart.

*Kill the bastards!!!*

(Official note – Capt Meroney's remark about not waiting to position yourself for a bounce is a bit over-eager. Every effort should be made to get into a good attack position short of losing the Hun.)

### Virgil K Meroney

Meroney was born on 16 February 1921 in Pine Bluff, Arkansas. During May 1937 he joined the Arkansas National Guard and was called to active duty during 1940, at which time he applied for flight training. Meroney was successful in his application and won his wings, and a commission as a second lieutenant, on 30 October 1942 at Luke Field.

Subsequently assigned to the 487th FS/352nd FG on 28 December 1942, Meroney headed with the group, and its Thunderbolts, to Britain during June 1943 – it began flying escort missions during September. Meroney scored his first aerial victory on 1 December, and became the group's first ace on 30 January 1944. While continuing to raise his score, he was shot down on 8 April 1944 by ground fire while strafing an airfield in Germany (by this time the unit had converted to the P-51B). Becoming a prisoner of war, Meroney escaped and managed to reach advancing American forces that were heading towards the Rhine.

After the war, he became a career USAF officer and flew F-84s in combat during the Korean War, followed by 141 combat missions in F-4 Phantom IIs during the Vietnam War. His son, Virgil K Meroney III, was listed as missing in action over Laos when his F-4D disappeared on 1 March 1969. Meroney senior retired as a colonel in December 1970, and died from cancer on 27 June 1980. His final tally was nine destroyed and one damaged.

Unlike most 352nd FG aces, Virgil Meroney scored all nine of his kills flying a Thunderbolt – P-47D-5 42-8473 to be precise! He became the group's first ace on 30 January 1944, and would have undoubtedly scored many more victories following his unit's transition to the P-51B had he not been shot down by flak whilst strafing an airfield in Germany on 8 April 1944. Having lost part of his left wing, and with his engine ablaze up to the firewall, Meroney bailed out just above the airfield, deploying his parachute as he vacated the Mustang. He was quickly captured and made a PoW (*via 352nd FG Association*)

Veteran P-47D-2 42-8390 finally ran out of luck when it attempted to land at its Raydon base on 22 April 1944. This aircraft was assigned to the 353rd FG's 352nd FS, and it featured the group's distinctive yellow and black chequered cowling. The pilot appears to have groundlooped and careered off the runway, digging a wing into the damp Raydon grass due to the sheer weight of the fighter. The P-47 has then performed a slow somersault onto its back. Fortunately for the pilot, the fighter has not burst into flames, allowing him to scramble out of the still structurally intact canopy (*via Michael O'Leary*)

# 1LT JESSE W GONNAM 352nd FS/353rd FG

Timing is a most essential part of defensive tactics against enemy aircraft which are in a bouncing position above the flight. At high operational altitudes I believe the P-47 can both out-turn and out-climb either the Me 109 or the Fw 190. If one knows his own and his aircraft's abilities, he can wait for the correct time to break up and into the enemy aircraft. This is strictly a matter of individual opinion, and I believe if the enemy aircraft are over 1000 yards away one can wait and break in plenty of time to drop behind the passing enemy aircraft which, in a high speed dive, cannot turn with the P-47. German aircraft have some bad characteristics at high speeds at high altitudes which should be used to the best advantage. Above 25,000 ft the P-47 can out-turn them either right or left, and at the same time gain enough altitude to put the pilot in a position to bounce.

Only when caught with one's head up and with an enemy aircraft

astern would I roll and try to out-dive the enemy aircraft, being rather rough on the controls and using every bad flying method available to prevent strikes on myself. A good sloppy aileron roll is a good evasive manoeuvre.

With the present additional power of the water injection system, one can outrun the enemy aircraft on the deck. Low clouds are very good cover and can be used. I also believe that at no time should one ever co-ordinate while there is an enemy astern, as this is really asking for it.

In a photograph no doubt posed specifically for the official USAAF photographer in attendance, Lt Will Jordan of the 352nd FS/353rd FG, is congratulated by his groundcrew after returning to Raydon from a successful mission. Shaking his hand is Assistant Crew Chief Sgt H L 'Gibby' Gibson, whilst the individual to his right is the aircraft's armourer, Sgt D W Knowlton. Finally, to Jordan's left is his crew chief, S/Sgt F W Robbsey. The P-47 behind them is adorned with no less than 48 mission markers in the form of crosses, plus two bomb symbols, two swastikas (signifying aerial kills) and a suitably 'Nazified' train silhouette. Note also the dice painted above the fighter's truly apt nickname (*via Michael O'Leary*)

The 352nd FS's Lt Mike Morrison poses alongside his uniquely marked P-47C Hi-Lander at Metfield in late 1943. Note the cover on the gunsight, the rear view mirror and the complex structure of the early Thunderbolt windscreen (via Michael O'Leary)

On several occasions the squadron has been bounced from above by superior numbers. Through the use of timing, and the flying advantage of the P-47, we came out on the offensive end with victories for us, and no losses. The methods described proved most effective. At no time would I sacrifice altitude or speed, as they are most essential to out-perform the enemy. The Hun is always in the sun, and a turn into the sun will often disrupt the plans of the Jerry. A head-on shot is a very poor position, and a good bluff will sometimes put the Hun on the defensive. Remember, I say sometimes!

In defensive tactics a wingman is one's best defence, for two pilots can trap and get the Hun by the old break and slide in behind the Hun method. A wingman who does his job well often gets the kills on the Jerry through good headwork. Nothing so reassures a pilot as to have his buddy or wingman stay with him and help him out.

P-47D-2 42-22475 of the 353rd FG returned to Metfield on 3 October 1943 with a tail section heavily damaged by enemy fire (*via Michael O'Leary*)

Yet another battle-damaged 353rd FG Thunderbolt, P-47D-15 42-76189 struggled back to Metfield, where its pilot carried out a textbook belly landing. This photograph reveals that the D-Day invasion stripes applied by some groups to their aircraft passed right around the fuselage. The turbosupercharger unit fitted in the underbelly of the P-47 also appears to have been partially ripped away by the impact of the landing

Maj Walter 'Turk' Beckham of the 351st FS/353rd FG was photographed with his groundcrew, and his Thunderbolt, at Metfield in late 1943. At the extreme left is assistant crew chief Sgt Marvin Eichstaedt, next to him armourer Sgt Richard Verity, then Beckham, and finally crew chief, S/Sgt Henry Bush. On 8 February 1944 he became the highest scoring Eighth Air Force ace when he downed a Bf 109 and an Fw 190 near St Hubert for his 17th and 18th confirmed victories. This particular fighter (P-47D-5 42-8476 *LITTLE DEMON*) was the only Thunderbolt known to have been assigned to him, and he was not flying it when shot down by flak gunners protecting Ostheim airfield, near Cologne, on 22 February 1944 (*via Bill Hess*)

The ability of an element to operate in pairs or a flight as elements is the key to all offensive attacks in my humble estimation. A good wingman is worth his weight in gold, and an element should fly enough together so that radio transmission conversation is unnecessary to plan or execute an attack.

If possible, bounces should be made from above and from out of the sun. Timing is again an essential factor in the attack. The enemy frequently half-rolls to evade with sufficient top cover and, under the present policy of destroying enemy aircraft, I would surely follow him down. On frequent occasions the Hun has rolled around in an Immelman to end up in a position to attack. This is one reason why I would follow him down. As a P-47 can out-dive the Hun, one can often complete a kill before placing himself too low to reform with the formation. Be wary of getting pulled down where the enemy can strike from behind. Remember always that the Jerry is a cunning, dangerous fighter, and that he uses every advantage given him. In turns at high altitude, one can out-turn the Jerry enough to get deflection.

Only under conditions of insufficient gas, and being outnumbered more than four-to-one, would I refrain from attack. Providing you had altitude and gas, you would have to be really outnumbered to refrain from an opportunity to destroy the enemy.

Seen here whilst still a captain, which dates this photograph as pre-December 1943, Walt Beckham had completed a tour in the Panama Canal Zone prior to joining the 353rd FG. He achieved 'acedom' on 10 October when he destroyed two Bf 110s and an 'Me 210' (almost certainly an Me 410) near Munster, and was made CO of the 351st FS the following month. Had Beckham not been downed by flak on 22 February 1944, it is likely that he would have been the first ace in the ETO – if not the whole USAAF – to have passed Eddie Rickenbacker's 26-kill mark set in 1918. Beckham's combat record was truly impressive, for he downed 18 German fighters in just 57 missions. Postwar, he remained in the USAF, rising to the rank of full colonel prior to retiring in 1969 (*via Bill Hess*)

I have often been guilty of overshooting the enemy. Of course, there is no simpler way to prevent this than to chop the throttle. If this doesn't work, a quick barrel roll will slow one down and put you in a position to fire again. Skidding is a good method. Once one has started an attack, and has a clear rear with good support above, I'd chase the Hun into the ground if that were possible. Some of these boys take a lot of shooting, and there is no

surer way of knowing the enemy aircraft is destroyed than to see the aeroplane hit the ground. It is also a very satisfying sight after one has been fired on a few times.

If possible, I would avoid deflection shots. The average pilot has a hard time hitting with a lot of deflection. Of course, there are often lucky hits that destroy the Jerry, but there is nothing so effective as a good astern shot. Head-on shots are hard, and should be avoided if anything else is possible.

I always break off combat in a tight, climbing turn, and have a good look behind, as the Jerry has a dirty habit of sliding in behind someone who is firing. That is where a wingman comes in, but often he too can be attacked. In this case you can clear his tail if you have broken combat properly and are alert. A pair of pilots who have flown together can easily box a single in, and then I say shoot him down regardless of who does the shooting. I certainly do not disapprove of wingmen firing at the enemy and, if the case arises when they are in position and

No doubt suffering from fatigue at the end of a long mission, the pilot of this 350th FS/353rd FG P-47D-6 (42-74672) applied the brakes a little too hard whilst taxying back to his dispersal and tipped the big fighter on to its nose. Bearing the sadly appropriate nickname of *EL SHAFTO*, the aircraft was photographed at Raydon on 24 May 1944. Note also the stencilling *HANDS OFF GUNS* applied to the fighter's wing leading edges (*via Michael O'Leary*)

**Above and below left**
This immaculate P-47D-21 was the personal mount of Col Glenn E Duncan, who was not only the CO of the 353rd FG from late November 1943 until he was shot down on 7 July 1944, but also the ranking ace of the group with 19.5 kills. Flying a series of fighters named the *Dove of Peace*, Duncan claimed all of his victories in the Thunderbolt. This particular P-47 was *Dove of Peace VI* (note the roman numerals to the right of 'X' in the fighter's code), and it had been delivered to the group in the late winter of 1944 finished in Olive Drab and dark grey. However, all camouflage paint was stripped off come the spring, and the bare aluminium skin waxed and buffed. Like most US aces downed in the ETO, Duncan was 'bagged' by flak whilst strafing an airfield – this time it was Wesendorf, and the colonel force-landed his P-47 near Nienburg. Evading capture, Duncan made it to Holland, where he joined the Dutch underground. He eventually returned to the 353rd FG in April 1945! (*both via Michael O'Leary*)

I am not, then I fly the wing to the wingmen, giving them protection. Some wingmen are damn fine shots and often lost a chance to score. Co-operation and an unselfish attitude can score more than any other known method.

The bounce can often be made by the flight leader, who is so designated by virtue of his experience and ability. There are times when the leader cannot bounce and the element can, so I say here and now that the flight leader should let the element lead the attack if he cannot see the enemy. The element of surprise is most essential, time a valuable factor, and no time should be wasted with long radio transmission calls to locate the enemy. Good eyes are one's most valuable possession. Recognition of the enemy is a must, and these two combined make it much easier to destroy the enemy.

These tactics must be carefully worked out by the individuals flying together and understood thoroughly, as there can be no breach of air discipline in a dogfight. Only a good understanding and constant practice can insure that a good flight will operate to its fullest perfection.

A fighter pilot is an individual, and his thoughts and actions must be complete and instantaneous. Often there can be no changing of decisions and, on the other hand, they often must be changed many times. Therefore, those gifted persons must be singled out to lead, and as leaders they must strive for perfection. The P-47 is a wonderful airplane and a very good gun platform, but the pilot makes the difference between a destroyed aeroplane or just a scared Jerry.

# MAJ EDWARD W SZANIAWSKI
## COMMANDING OFFICER
## 357th FS/355th FG

If a squadron flies well and the flights stay compactly one on the other, very few attacks will occur. If the Hun is foolish enough to stick his neck out under these conditions, the attacks can be easily dispersed. If less than a squadron is involved, it goes back to the same old story – a good lookout and a great into the attack plan.

The pilot must stay calm and take advantage of all breaks. He must try to stay together if possible and disperse the Hun. Once they are broken up they fight as individuals, which under ordinary conditions gives us quite an advantage.

When attacked, fight like hell, try to stay together, and work toward the coast. If a last resort is necessary, hit the deck and go like hell. When caught on the deck, there is not much one can do except fight it out or try to run.

Generally, I would hit the deck only when attacked by vastly superior forces, or gas or ammunition are low, or in case of engine trouble or lack of oxygen. It is always advisable, however, to try to maintain some altitude when coming out.

In most of my encounters the enemy always went for the deck, thus turning the fight into a plain old rat race until the enemy pulled out. In all encounters where one must concentrate on the enemy (whether twin- or single-engined fighters), it is absolutely essential that the wingman cover the leader. If the leader can give his wingman a chance to shoot, for example, when the enemy is completely surprised, by all means let him join in the fight. This type of teamwork is surely good for morale.

Unless the enemy is surprised, he usually breaks into the attack, or half rolls and heads for the deck. If the enemy aircraft hold their altitude, the pilot should pick out one and concentrate on him until he is destroyed. If he heads for the deck, the same holds good. The pilot should always pick out one and follow through. He should always attack if gas and ammunition are sufficient. If the enemy is hit hard, even by fewer numbers, it usually results in his dispersion. From then on pilots must stick together and get the individuals.

The first CO of the 355th FG's 357th FS, Edward Szaniawski was just a first lieutenant when given command of the all new unit in February 1943. He remained in charge of the squadron until 20 May 1944, when his P-51B was shot down by flak and he was made a PoW. By then Szaniawski had claimed four aerial kills (two of these were achieved on 11 February 1944), one probable and two damaged, as well as 4.66 strafing victories (*via Bill Hess*)

By concentration on the individual attacked, under normal conditions overshooting can be avoided. However, under certain conditions with the P-47 it's very hard to keep from overshooting a good enemy pilot who knows the ropes. The best way is to plan a little ahead and to use discretion until he is destroyed.

In general, most young pilots are just fair shots. This can be overcome by a dead astern approach and closing as near as possible before one opens fire. However, I believe snap deflection shots are justified if one is unable to get into a stern position. I try not to shoot unless the range is favourable. It's foolish to waste ammunition. A little study now and again on this subject never hurt anyone.

As for formation, en route from enemy coast to rendezvous point, the three squadrons fly abreast, built up away from the sun in two steps of 1000 to 2000 ft. Each squadron thus covers the others, and a large area is covered. Squadron formation is two flights of four – one section flying abreast, with the second section 100 to 200 yards behind it and 500 to a 1000 ft above.

The dispersion of squadrons usually depends upon the mission involved. Generally speaking, under present conditions I favour one squadron to the rear of bombers, one in front and the third as high cover. I like the flights within the squadron in a trail formation during escort, each flight 300 to 400 yards behind the other. In the flights, I like elements and wingmen 25 to 50 yards apart, and well up in an abreast formation. This affords mutual cross-over protection and manoeuvrability.

Squadrons should attempt to maintain close contact with one another at all times, although it is not always possible if many enemy aircraft are present. However, I require my flights to keep very close contact with the squadron. This is accomplished by radio transmission announcing bounces, etc. The range around bombers is very elastic, depending on the type of mission and activity of enemy aircraft in the vicinity. If bombers are happy, range or area is of course much greater than otherwise. Victories pay off it seems, so we go hunting.

On normal escort missions any flight in the squadron is allowed, and encouraged, to make a bounce. Flight leaders call in their bounces and get cover from the nearest flight as the situation demands. For example, if the second flight makes a bounce, the first flight can cover, or vice versa. If a section is required for a bounce, one section should cover the other as long as possible.

Flights should try to stick together, whilst at the same time be flexible. It is perfectly all right for the second element to make a bounce, but in such cases the first element should cover the bounce. There is strength in numbers, and sticking together invariably pays off in the long run.

Our four flights fly in trail formation during escort, 300 to 500 yards apart. This gives good protection to bombers, provides cover over a large area, the flights offer each other mutual protection and the squadron has great manoeuvrability. Furthermore, this formation is easy on all pilots involved, and encourages a good look-out. For sweeps, two flights fly abreast, about 500 yards apart, with the other two flights abreast 500 to 1000 yards behind them.

Some 300 P-47D-5s were built by Republic in New York in 1943, and this aircraft (42-8404) was number two off the production line. Assigned to the 355th FG's 354th FS at Steeple Morden, it was the regular mount of a Lt Col T Hubbard (*via Bill Hess*)

With new pilots constantly joining the organisation, certain rigid rules must be established for efficient operation. Under present conditions, the type of formation we fly is very satisfactory in this theatre. It is flexible and manoeuvrable enough if pilots are trained properly, and enables flight leaders to maintain good air discipline.

If flights, and the men in them, are in there proper position and on the ball, most defensive situations with the enemy in a position to attack can be handled effectively and without loss. In fact, the tables are often reversed, and one or more victories result. The Hun seems reluctant to pick on flights or sections, but God help the stragglers. This seems to apply even when he has a definite advantage.

The size of the enemy formations influences all bounces. If a flight is all that is necessary, it is despatched with top cover. If the situation requires more, a section or even the whole squadron makes the bounce. It is always desirable to seek numerical advantage. However, even without numerical superiority, a bounce should be made at every opportunity, and in most cases the average Hun will make a wrong move and get his pants burned.

We drop belly tanks only when attacked by the enemy, or when an attack is being made by us. In all cases try to hold tanks as long as possible on penetration. That 20 or 30 gallons saved looks good on the long flight home.

Some of the Huns can really make a '190 talk, but in general it's the same old stuff in new equipment.

Pilots should circle the area of combat and climb gently until men have the chance to reform and rejoin the squadron. If still with the bombers, use of the radio to state one's immediate position makes it easier for men to rejoin.

After group briefing I again brief the squadron. We go over our part of the picture, the type of formation for the mission, weather conditions, and all other little facts of immediate importance. This makes it easier on all concerned, for everyone then knows what to expect of the leader. I find this only takes a few minutes, and is very helpful.

I would order a formation to hit the deck only if attacked and the squadron was very low on gas or ammunition. If a member or members of a flight are in trouble and cannot maintain altitude, the flight should stay together and help them home. If coming out under a solid overcast at low altitudes and in vicinity of large towns, sometimes flights like to come out on the deck in order to avoid the heavy flak. In this case, leaders usually allow men to decide by radio whether or not to go down to the deck.

Leaders should try to give bounces to men who are in the best position to bounce. Of course it's hard to see everything, so flights are most often despatched. After that it's up to the flight leader involved as to who okays the bounces.

The enemy aircraft involved, and also the type of mission, determine the number of our aircraft sent down on a bounce. On escort, if one flight can handle the situation, it's foolish to use the whole squadron and leave the bombers unprotected. On sweeps, a squadron can more easily work as a unit under all conditions.

When the enemy has advantage of altitude and position, pilots must try to stay close together, gain altitude and turn the tables. By all means they must keep close watch on all his movements and wait for him to make a move. All the while they should try to obtain a more favourable position. Often times even if the Hun attacks from above, the tables can be turned in short order if he has been watched carefully. This is especially so with P-47s, for the Hun doesn't like head-on attacks with this ship.

We try to pursue attacks until a victory is obtained. If necessary, and usually it is, we pursue from the bombers right down to the deck.

By all means pilots should try to make an attack before the Hun can get set on the bombers. They should keep the enemy dispersed and away from the bombers as much as possible. If they range around bombers ten miles or so in either direction, most attacks can usually be stopped before they are started.

Pilots should range in all directions away from the bombers. Leaders should keep the squadron together as long as possible, and they should sweep their area to both sides. For example, if the pilot is in the front squadron, he should sweep this area from side to side, always keeping

The 355th FG arrived in England in July 1943 and commenced operations in mid-September. Although the date on which this line-up shot was taken has been lost to history, judging by the unmarked white cowling bands and freshly-applied red-ringed 'star and bars', these P-47Ds were photographed basking in the late summer sun at Steeple Morden in August 1943. The following month the 355th was committed to a punishing cycle of combat missions that continued unabated through to May 1945, and these aircraft soon lost their parade ground appearance (*via Bill Hess*)

close tabs on the bombers by vision or radio transmission. Often by keeping the escort elastic, many aeroplanes can be engaged in the general area, and still good escort provided. This also keeps the enemy from hanging around outside the escort until an attack is possible.

If possible, all flights call in bounces to the squadron leader before leaving the squadron formation. They are then despatched. However, if time does not allow, flights can make bounces and announce their intentions on the way down. Elements can make bounces also, but where possible I try to keep the flight together, one element covering the other. Never break the squadron down into less than elements if possible.

The best offensive is in keeping together and hitting hard. The best defence is also maintained by sticking together and by trying to disperse the enemy and turning the tide. The best tactic in any case is trying to maintain altitude, but if this is impossible, take the action to the tree tops if necessary.

Flight leaders always make the bounces if time permits. If an element leader bounces, he must notify his flight leader at once.

If necessary to drop down to the deck or to low altitude to evade an attack or because of mechanical difficulties, re-climb to 8000 ft as soon as possible in order to avoid light and heavy flak.

## MAJ JAMES H THORNE
## 359th FS/356th FG

When an individual pilot is attacked by enemy aircraft, the most important thing is to do something violent, and to do it quickly.

In an element travelling alone, the wingman should stay with the element leader unless told on the radio transmission to break and start co-ordinated defensive tactics.

I do not believe that a pilot should remain on the deck except when actually under attack, or for camouflage reasons. To remain on the deck makes navigation poor, restricts the area of vision and leaves the pilot open to automatic weapons fire from the ground.

When the element leader is making an attack I believe the wingman should stay slightly behind and higher than the element leader. If possible he should be off to one side, but quite often manoeuvring precludes this. Enemy single-engined aircraft almost always use a descending manoeuvre for defence which I cannot understand, because it is the one time a P-47 really has performance over enemy aircraft. A good enemy pilot will keep you from hitting him until you arrive at the deck. As long as he has altitude to manoeuvre with, he will go through a whole series of manoeuvres that effectively make him an extremely poor target.

Numbers, as such, do not very greatly enter in offensive tactics. Altitude makes the attacking of superior numbers very profitable.

In firing at enemy aircraft, except for purely defensive firing, I would never take a shot over 15 degrees deflection. Although the enemy aircraft may look as though you are dead astern, there is a very great probability that you are not – therefore allow some deflection.

The condition of the P-47C-2s and D-1s seen in this line-up shot contrasts markedly with the prisitine fighters of the 355th FG seen on page 69. These Thunderbolts are from the 78th FG's 82nd FS, and they are seen parked at their dispersal on a muddy Duxford airfield in December 1943 – note the 'stray' Lancaster being worked on in amongst the American fighters. The aircraft parked third from the camera is P-47D-1 42-7954, which was used by future six-kill ace James Wilkinson to claim his first victory (a Bf 109G) on 1 December 1943. He would eventually become CO of the 82nd FS on 18 May 1944, although his command of the unit would last just 17 days, for he was killed when his P-47D-22 (42-26256) crashed near Llandovery, in South Wales, on 4 June (*via Bill Hess*)

We use a very tight formation from take off to just before landfall. This formation has been found to save a considerable amount of gasoline on the part of the number four men of the squadron. From just prior to crossing the enemy coast up to the rendezvous point, we fly sections line abreast, with the individual aircraft line abreast. Although this formation is not very manoeuvrable, as a formation, it is very good defensively, and frequent turns are not expected prior to rendezvous.

Flights have individual initiative as to initiating attacks anytime, anywhere. The attack is generally made by whoever sees the enemy aircraft first. Almost never will the squadron leader have time to detail a specific flight or element to make an attack.

Very rarely will the flights be able to join the squadron after making an attack. Where it is possible for the flight to rejoin, it should do so. If it is impossible for the flight to rejoin, it should either start home or join another squadron.

Recently, within our own organisation, we have tended towards smaller combat units, that is, permitting a flight of four ships to have more freedom of action. An element of two is the absolute lowest division for combat, and a four-ship section is very desirable.

On a normal bounce the man seeing the enemy aircraft, whether he is a wingman, element leader, or section leader, makes the attack. He is covered by his flight. The other four-ship flight stays above the flight long enough to be certain that no more enemy aircraft will join the fight from above.

As to individual initiative in beginning attacks, standard practice does not permit a wingman to attack if his leader sees the enemy. An over-anxious or badly disciplined wingman can easily mess up an attack.

# 1Lt C A Vitali
# 360th FS/356th FG

I received your letter today requesting my personal points of view on combat tactics and am answering immediately in the hope of being of some assistance to you.

Firstly, concerning individual combat tactics when on the defensive. If I were being attacked from dead astern by superior numbers, I would break immediately and violently to the side and down, and would keep going either into a layer of cloud, thereupon changing my course, or straight to the deck. If, on the other hand, I were attacked by a single enemy aircraft, I would break in the same manner but would not continue down, but rather would pick up enough speed for a good zoom and would pull back up as steeply as possible, and there wing-over into a tight turn at the top. After that, I believe, I would be on the offensive.

If attacked from the quarter or beam I would turn into the enemy aircraft and, if unable to meet him head-on, I would always turn in the direction from which he were coming, never the opposite, in order to engage him in a circle with the hope of out-turning him, or at least giving him a very difficult shot. I find that the tightest turn may be obtained in a pinch by putting the prop in very fine pitch with manual control if necessary, lowering about ten degrees of flaps and trimming the ship in the turn. If ever bounced by superior numbers while on the deck, the only possible thing left is evasive action by zooming, diving, corkscrewing, skidding, etc. If on the other hand I were attacked by a single enemy aircraft on the deck, I would immediately go into a steep turn and try to out-turn him.

Some aeroplanes – the Fw 190 for one – have a very violent steep-turn stall characteristic. Consequently, their pilots are either timid about turning too sharply, or they make the fatal mistake of reefing it in and snap-stalling on the deck. I would never hit the deck unless attacked by superior numbers, or as a last resort, as altitude is most valuable, and when lost is hard to regain.

When on the offensive and attacking a superior force, I would use only the hit and run method of attack, making one swift pass from above and astern and continuing on through and down. I consider it inadvisable to attack such a force from the same level, from below or from any angle but astern, as they would be able to turn into you and would also have as much speed, or more, with which to overtake you. On the other hand, when making a surprise attack on a single enemy aircraft, or slightly superior force, I would get to the astern position and slightly below (a perfectly blind spot) as fast as possible, and would then throttle back to almost his speed to prevent overshooting, and at the same time allow myself to trim and take perfect aim.

I would try not to fire at all from out of range, lest I warn him of my approach, but rather would get as close as possible and then open up and hold it for a sure thing. In making a deflection shot I would fire short bursts, observing the results, if any, of each burst and making a correction after each burst if necessary. When I finally got what I was after, then I would bear down on the trigger. I believe the best position for a wingman to fly is well out and well up almost line abreast, thus assuring perfect cross-cover, and making it impossible for an enemy aircraft to make a hit-run attack on both ships.

Concerning formation combat tactics, we have found that from the form-up throughout the climb to the enemy coast, the easiest squadron formation to fly is a tight one, as it tends to eliminate the dropping behind of single ships, elements, or flights, consequently eliminating large boost corrections to catch up.

When altitude or the enemy coast is reached, then three of the four flights spread out as near line abreast as possible, as do the elements. The fourth flight continues climbing to a position 3000 or 4000 ft above and up-sun from the rest of the unit to break up any possible attack on the squadron, or to cover any attacks made by the squadron.

When escorting the bombers, the formation changes to four flights in trail, which travel alongside and up-sun from the bombers, and in the same direction as the bombers. As each flight in succession passes the front of the bombers, it makes an orbit around to the end of the line and repeats the process. The advantages of this type of escort are that it eliminates cross-weaving, thus allowing more attention to be paid to the bombers, other aircraft or the sun. It enables the aeroplanes to maintain more speed (a very important thing), and each flight has a flight before and behind it at all times, and also a flight going in the opposite direction toward the rear of the bombers. Thus everyone is covered at all times from all directions.

Except in the case of an organised attack on a formation of enemy aircraft, in which the squadron leader delegates a flight or an element to attack, any flight or element is free to make a bounce, providing the leader making the bounce calls it on his way down so that he may be covered, or at least later accounted for.

Wingmen should never peel off on their own, as elements should be kept intact as long as possible so that element leaders may be covered while attacking and shooting, and also for defensive reasons. When attacking a twin-engined aircraft in the vicinity of bombers, a top cover for the attack on it is particularly important, as these twin-engined aircraft almost invariably have their own private escort covering them from up-sun. One squadron, or at least a flight or two, out of a group escorting bombers should fly at the same level, or below, the bombers, and out of sight of the top cover.

If I were leading a flight and saw a flight of enemy aircraft which had an advantage of altitude and position, I would start a fast climb away from them without turning my back to them until I got to their level. Then I would start toward them, still climbing until close enough for a bounce. I would pursue an attack to the limit, providing the bombers had some cover left, and gas permitting.

The most effective way to break up an attack by enemy aircraft that have already started for the bombers is to make yourself seen by getting in front and turning into them and firing guns regardless of aim, rather than follow them down after they have attacked the bombers.

I hope that these personal opinions and ideas are more or less what you wanted. If at anytime I can be of some service, I will be very happy to co-operate.

# Lt Col William Waller III
# Commanding Officer
# 361st FS/356th FG

In response to your letter, I will endeavour to express what I consider a few pertinent thoughts on air combat and air tactics. In proportion to my limited combat experience, my opinions on combat tactics must also be limited. I have only made 74 sorties for 39 trips into enemy territory, and have only been engaged infrequently with enemy fighters.

Of the utmost importance is the ability of the wingman to stick to his element leader regardless of the violence of manoeuvres. Two pilots together can employ any number of tactics or tricks to protect each other. One, alone, has no protection against superior numbers, and can only hope to out-fly his opponents with the odds in their favour.

Likewise, sections, flights and squadrons afford the individual more protection against both surprise attack and enemy fire in the clear, as well as providing more firepower to use against the enemy when you have him where you can reach him. *Always* endeavour to keep the squadron in the same piece of sky, but *never* let the wingman get separated from his leader.

The decision to make a bounce must be made practically instantaneously. If you are going to fire your guns at all, you must go the instant you see the bounce, and not waste time trying to position yourself just right or you won't get to shoot. If you don't like the look of the situation, send a small part of your force to bounce and use the rest to cover it, *but well!* You may all get to shoot if you do it right, but if you don't do it instantly, no one will get a shot.

If possible, always provide yourself with upper cover when you are going to go down on something. Once you have seen him, don't let him get between you and the sun if you can prevent it.

When he is on your tail, don't panic – that's easy enough to do!

Literally sat on top of his P-47D, which he named *SKEETER-KISS OF DEATH*, Lt Col William Waller III shares a joke with his groundcrew. CO of the 356th FG's 361st FS from 26 November 1943 through to 16 July 1944, his final official score was one shared kill and 1.5 damaged (*via Tom Frisque*)

Use all the evasive action you can think of and he won't hit you once out of a hundred rounds. At the same time, try to have a look around and see if you can't find a friend, then lead him over there. Your friend will be only too glad to knock him off your tail if you can get to him. Two P-47 pilots, who were being hard pressed by a couple of '109s, did just that for me recently. Led them right up in front of my nose and gave me some very nice shooting. The kind of thing fighter pilots daydream about!

If you want to get home and try it again another day, you had better have a full knowledge of *all* radio transmitter facilities, and how to use them *properly*.

A thorough understanding of *all* your emergency equipment, and how to use it properly, is excellent life insurance.

## COL THOMAS J J CHRISTIAN JR
## COMMANDING OFFICER
## 361st FG

In answering your request for my ideas concerning combat tactics, I am afraid that I would be forced to give you more theory about *individual* combat tactics than actual experience. My combats so far have been very few, and short-lived.

I have, however, led enough missions and seen enough enemy aircraft (which somebody else in the group always seems to bounce before I can get to them) to have a few ideas about *formation* combat tactics.

In general, our formations run something like this – from take-off to about three minutes before we hit the enemy coast, we fly a very tight four-ship V-formation. Individual elements, flights and the two low squadrons fly as close together as possible. We do this to keep the group together in poor visibility, and to conserve gas.

As we reach the enemy coast, we assume battle formation, whereupon individual ships move out to an easily manoeuvrable and mutually supporting distance, and come up line abreast within flights. Each man is constantly turning very slightly from this point on. Our squadron formation is a box of four flights, each flight flying line abreast. The second section flies roughly two to three hundred feet above the first section.

Upon contact with the bombers, the group leader positions squadrons by radio transmission, depending upon the size of the bomber formation, cloud cover, the type of bomber formation, the number of stragglers, the sun, etc. Our flights generally fly 500 to 800 yards apart when escorting bombers.

At the beginning of our operational experience, my primary objective was to keep the group together, and to keep the squadrons together until sections and flights had enough experience to take care of themselves. I feel that we have had that experience by now and, consequently, we do not stress keeping together as a squadron as much now as formerly. I am very much in favour of a more highly ranging looser type of formation, provided the flights are experienced enough to take care of themselves. It is only in this manner that we are able to find the Hun before some other groups pick him off.

As far as defensive action is concerned, I am of the opinion that the line abreast formation is best for both defensive and offensive work. We never drop our belly tanks until we see enemy aircraft definitely committing themselves to an attack on our formation. After combat, the group or squadron generally assembles on the bombers, or on a particular box of bombers, over some prominent landmark, or by flying a given course and then orbiting.

The only time that I would order my formation to hit the deck as a defensive measure would be when we were short of gas and attacked by overwhelming numbers, out of ammunition, etc. I do not believe in bringing a formation out on the deck if it can possibly be avoided.

As far as offensive tactics are concerned, bounces are determined by a combination of the circumstances – who sees the enemy aircraft first, who is in the best position to bounce, how important it is that the group make its R/V, the number of enemy aircraft to be bounced, etc.

In general, I believe it is best to let the person who sees the enemy aircraft first make the bounce. We have lost a lot of Huns trying to give directions to some other flight as to their location. Flight and element leaders always call in their bounces, but not necessarily before they make the bounce. Under the present tactical policy, I do not believe that the distance of enemy aircraft away from the bombers makes any difference in the decision as to whether or not to attack them. At the present time, bombers are, figuratively speaking, 'bait to attract the Hun'.

As for my own recommendations, I am not in favour of large 'on the deck' missions. I believe that we should go over at altitude, say 10,000 ft, pick out a target, drop down so that the formation can follow some definite landmarks to the target, such as rivers or highways, make one pass and then gradually regain altitude. Co-ordinated attacks on one target could be made by flights or sections in this manner.

Most groups range or spread out more after a little experience in order to spot and hit the Hun before he attacks the bombers.

Belly tanks are also dropped when they are dry.

Although scoring no aerial kills, Col Thomas J Christian Jr was nevertheless an inspirational leader to his men. The only West Point graduate to command a fighter group in the ETO, Christian was placed in charge of the 361st FG upon its activation in February 1943. He oversaw the group's training on the P-47 in the USA, then led it into combat in January 1944. Transitioning with the 361st onto the Mustang in May, Christian remained in the thick of the action until he was shot down and killed (in P-51D-5 44-13410) by flak while strafing a railroad marshalling yard in France on 12 August 1944 (*via Bill Hess*)

# P-38 LIGHTNING PILOTS

### Lt Col Mark E Hubbard
### Commanding Officer
### 20th FG

In answer to your letter, here are my personal comments on fighter tactics. Before answering some of your specific suggestions, I'll put down what I believe to be general tactics. Leadership, formation and control of the unit are all important: leadership, to plan on the ground and direct in the air; formation, to see the enemy, attack him and defend yourself; control, to attack in force at the proper time.

I won't attempt to explain leadership here, as that would take several pages in itself. Suffice it to say that it can only be acquired through experience and constant thought.

Formation is the line of battle which can be offensive or defensive as the situation requires (and the situation can change almost instantaneously). I am flat out for a line abreast formation, with flights spaced far enough apart for neutral aid. This spacing would vary from 800 to 1500 yards depending on the aeroplane's manoeuvrability. Squadrons

The official USAAF caption for this photograph read as follows; 'England – Lockheed P-38s stream through the thin atmosphere at their rendezvous point where they met the heavy bombers and escorted them on the bombing mission. These darting flashing denizens of the rarified high altitude atmosphere scored many victories whilst escorting the bombers over Europe' (*via John Stanaway*)

should be within good visual distance, meaning not more than two to three miles apart. Line abreast formation is as offensive as any other type, and defensively the best. You must see before you hit, or are hit.

Control can be maintained with radio transmission if squadrons or units are within eyesight. No mission can be planned to the finest detail on the ground, so the group leader must have control in order to use his force to the best advantage when the situation is met. On the other hand, a well defined plan should be made and understood by each pilot to aid in performing the mission and maintaining control in the event radio transmission should fail, which is always a possibility.

A most important consideration is 'know your aeroplane'. Use its advantages against the enemy, and keep those advantages by knowing its disadvantages. Every aircraft is superior or inferior in some respects to the enemy aeroplanes. Thank God ours are more superior than inferior. To know your aeroplane, keep training – and be continuous.

Superiority in numbers is all-important. That is where control comes in. Use your force as necessary, but always despatch enough.

Now to put down a few distracted points without regard for their order of importance, as all are important.

**A.** A wingman should always stay with his leader. Under no circumstances should there be less than two aeroplanes working together as one man cannot protect his own tail, and 90 per cent of all fighters shot down never saw the guy who hit them.

P-38J-15 43-104308 *'Gentle Annie'* was the mount of Col Harold J Rau, commanding officer of the 20th FG. He is seen here posing with his groundcrew (from left to right), T/Sgt James A Douglas, Sgt Grant L Beach and S/Sgt Luther W Ghent, and his dog Honey at King's Cliffe in mid April 1944. Rau assumed command of the group on 20 March 1944, and he was in turn relieved by Lt Col C Wilson at the end of June. He then took charge again on 27 August following the loss of his successor over Germany (Wilson was made a PoW). Rau remained CO until 18 December, when he came to the end of his extended tour in the ETO. Fitted with external tanks, the CO's P-38J has had its nose cone polished in the hope that Luftwaffe pilots would think that the aircraft was an unarmed photo-recce Lightning. Harry Rau scored all five of his kills (one Bf 109G shot down and four twin-engined aircraft strafed) during a single mission on 8 April 1944 (*via Michael O'Leary*)

The 20th FG's Lt V J Noble (far right bottom row) and his groundcrew pose in front of their heavily weathered, and decorated, P-38J-10 42-67449 *MiSS MASS* at King's Cliffe during the early spring of 1944. Reading the aircraft's mission log, three umbrellas denote a trio of top cover sorties completed, the eight top hat and sticks symbolise bomber escort missions (as do the bomb symbols) and the ten brooms fighter sweeps. Noble is not listed as a fighter ace, so the three swastikas may denote strafing kills or aerial successes claimed by other pilots in *MiSS MASS*. Note the P-38 engine cowlings scattered in the background (*via Michael O'Leary*)

An enthusiastic Lightning pilot from the 20th FG beats up a nearby B-24 base in East Anglia upon returning from a combat mission (*via Michael O'Leary*)

**B.** It is preferable that the minimum number of aircraft working together is a flight of four.

**C.** Each pilot should know what is expected of him in no uncertain terms. Leave no room for doubt.

**D.** Instrument training is essential, both individual and as members of a flight. Emphasis should be placed on recovery from spirals, spins, and stalls, and smooth straight and level flying.

Now to get on to answering some of your specific suggestions. These answers are numbered as in your letter. The specific aircraft in this case is the P-38J.

## Individual Combat Tactics

### DEFENSIVE

1. The P-38 will out turn any enemy fighter in the air up to 25,000 ft, so we wait until he is about one-half to one mile in back of us and then turn into him. Flights on either side may be despatched to attack if time permits.

2. After the turn we generally can attack him. If he zooms up, we climb until he breaks down, when we attack. If we cannot out climb him we continue on our course (opened up, line abreast) and let him make another pass if he so desires. Eventually, he will break down and we attack.

3. We always approach on the up sun side. Use cloud cover for defence only, which is damn seldom except with a cripple.

4. When the enemy attacks, we out turn him and continue on course always in line abreast opened up formation so we support each other. We hit the deck only as a last resort because then you are combating enemy fighters and light flak – personally, I'll take the fighters as I can see them and fight them. Hitting the deck is a good manoeuvre in open unprotected country, but not in well-populated well-protected country such as *Festung Europa*. On the deck you never know when you'll bust right over some well-protected target or airdrome. I believe light flak has accounted for one-half of all missing fighters who hit the deck (*text continues on page 97*).

The Lightning's nose-mounted quartet of 0.50-cal machine guns and solitary 20 mm cannon made the Lockheed fighter a formidable opponent for the Luftwaffe's equally well-armed Bf 109Gs and Fw 190s. Here, armourers get to grips with reloading empty 0.50-cal magazines on a 20th FG P-38H in the early spring of 1944 (*via Sam Sox*)

# Colour Plates

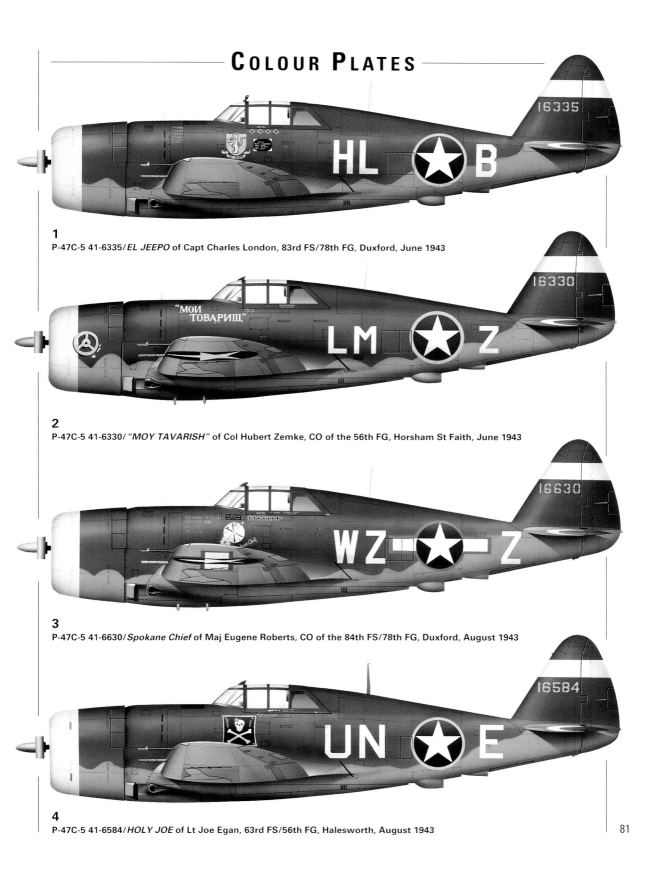

**1**
P-47C-5 41-6335/*EL JEEPO* of Capt Charles London, 83rd FS/78th FG, Duxford, June 1943

**2**
P-47C-5 41-6330/*"MOY TAVARISH"* of Col Hubert Zemke, CO of the 56th FG, Horsham St Faith, June 1943

**3**
P-47C-5 41-6630/*Spokane Chief* of Maj Eugene Roberts, CO of the 84th FS/78th FG, Duxford, August 1943

**4**
P-47C-5 41-6584/*HOLY JOE* of Lt Joe Egan, 63rd FS/56th FG, Halesworth, August 1943

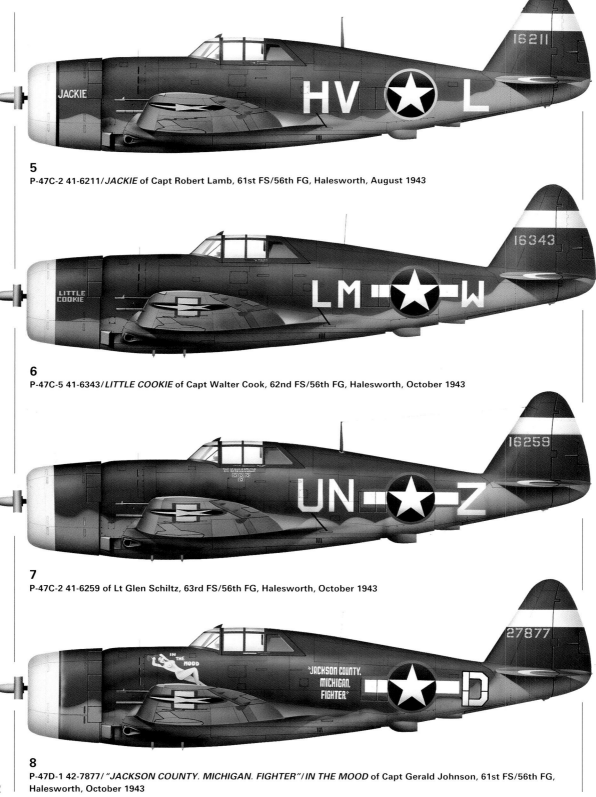

**5**
P-47C-2 41-6211/*JACKIE* of Capt Robert Lamb, 61st FS/56th FG, Halesworth, August 1943

**6**
P-47C-5 41-6343/*LITTLE COOKIE* of Capt Walter Cook, 62nd FS/56th FG, Halesworth, October 1943

**7**
P-47C-2 41-6259 of Lt Glen Schiltz, 63rd FS/56th FG, Halesworth, October 1943

**8**
P-47D-1 42-7877/*"JACKSON COUNTY. MICHIGAN. FIGHTER"*/*IN THE MOOD* of Capt Gerald Johnson, 61st FS/56th FG, Halesworth, October 1943

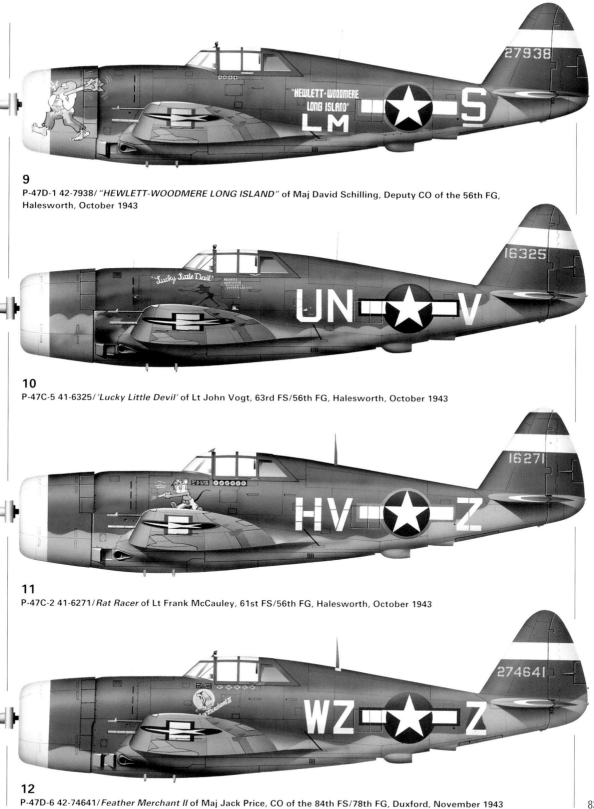

**9**
P-47D-1 42-7938/ *"HEWLETT-WOODMERE LONG ISLAND"* of Maj David Schilling, Deputy CO of the 56th FG, Halesworth, October 1943

**10**
P-47C-5 41-6325/ *'Lucky Little Devil'* of Lt John Vogt, 63rd FS/56th FG, Halesworth, October 1943

**11**
P-47C-2 41-6271/ *Rat Racer* of Lt Frank McCauley, 61st FS/56th FG, Halesworth, October 1943

**12**
P-47D-6 42-74641/ *Feather Merchant II* of Maj Jack Price, CO of the 84th FS/78th FG, Duxford, November 1943

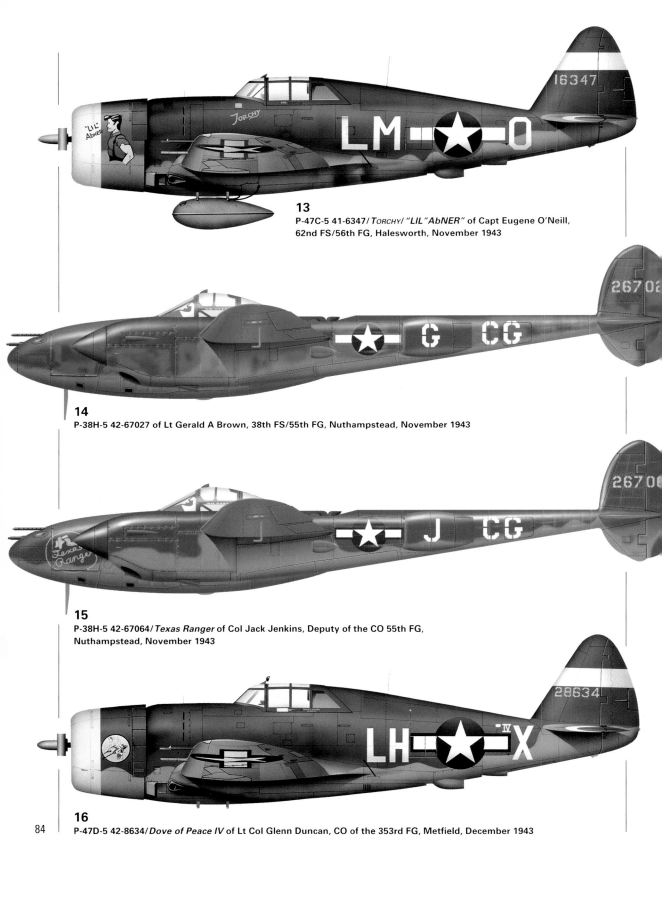

**13**
P-47C-5 41-6347 / *Torchy* / *"LIL "AbNER"* of Capt Eugene O'Neill,
62nd FS/56th FG, Halesworth, November 1943

**14**
P-38H-5 42-67027 of Lt Gerald A Brown, 38th FS/55th FG, Nuthampstead, November 1943

**15**
P-38H-5 42-67064 / *Texas Ranger* of Col Jack Jenkins, Deputy of the CO 55th FG,
Nuthampstead, November 1943

**16**
P-47D-5 42-8634 / *Dove of Peace IV* of Lt Col Glenn Duncan, CO of the 353rd FG, Metfield, December 1943

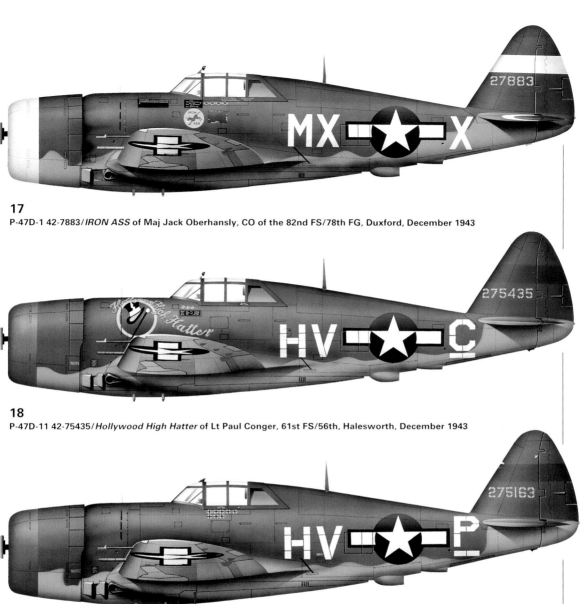

**17**
P-47D-1 42-7883/*IRON ASS* of Maj Jack Oberhansly, CO of the 82nd FS/78th FG, Duxford, December 1943

**18**
P-47D-11 42-75435/*Hollywood High Hatter* of Lt Paul Conger, 61st FS/56th, Halesworth, December 1943

**19**
P-47D-10 42-75163 of Lt Joe Powers, 61st FS/56th FG,
Halesworth, December 1943

**20**
P-47D-5 42-8476/*LITTLE DEMON* of Capt Walter Beckham, 351st FS/353rd FG, Metfield, December 1943

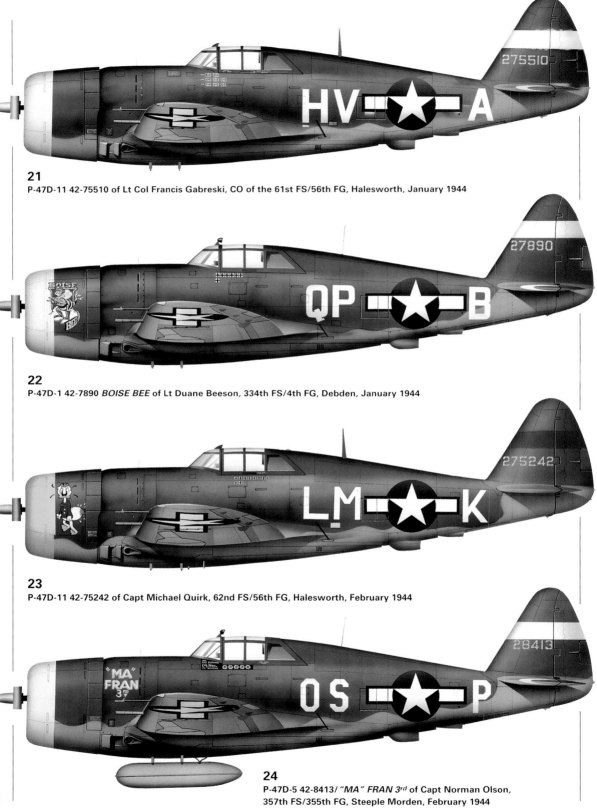

**21**
P-47D-11 42-75510 of Lt Col Francis Gabreski, CO of the 61st FS/56th FG, Halesworth, January 1944

**22**
P-47D-1 42-7890 *BOISE BEE* of Lt Duane Beeson, 334th FS/4th FG, Debden, January 1944

**23**
P-47D-11 42-75242 of Capt Michael Quirk, 62nd FS/56th FG, Halesworth, February 1944

**24**
P-47D-5 42-8413/ *"MA" FRAN 3rd* of Capt Norman Olson,
357th FS/355th FG, Steeple Morden, February 1944

**25**
P-47D-5 42-8461/"Lucky" of Lt Robert Johnson, 61st FS/56th FG, Halesworth, February 1944

**26**
P-38J-10 42-67717/My Dad of Capt James M Morris, 77th FS/20th FG, King's Cliffe, February 1944

**27**
P-47D-5 42-8487/"SPIRIT OF ATLANTIC CITY, N.J." of Capt Walker Mahurin, 63rd FS/56th FG, Halesworth,
March 1944

**28**
P-47D-5 42-8473 Sweet LOUISE/Mrs Josephine/Hedy of Capt Virgil Meroney, 487th FS/352nd FG, Bodney, March 1944

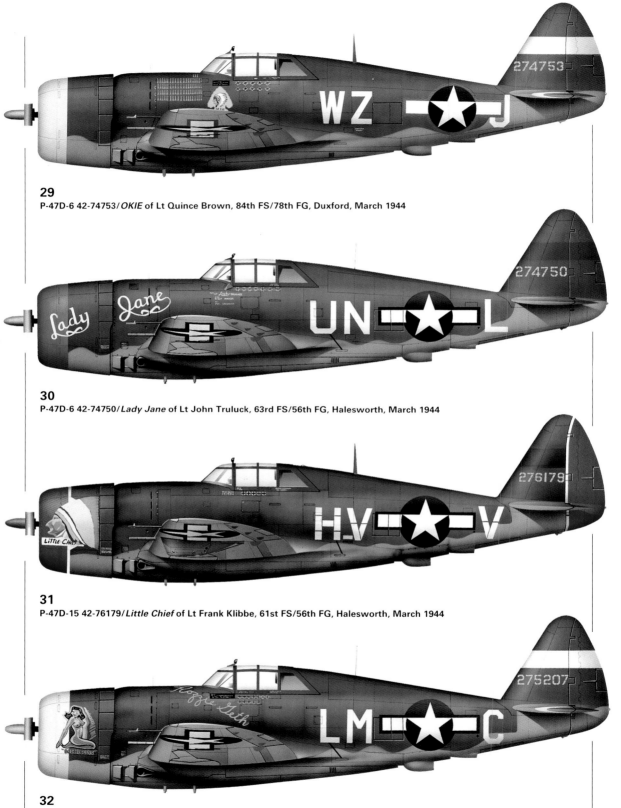

**29**
P-47D-6 42-74753/*OKIE* of Lt Quince Brown, 84th FS/78th FG, Duxford, March 1944

**30**
P-47D-6 42-74750/*Lady Jane* of Lt John Truluck, 63rd FS/56th FG, Halesworth, March 1944

**31**
P-47D-15 42-76179/*Little Chief* of Lt Frank Klibbe, 61st FS/56th FG, Halesworth, March 1944

**32**
P-47D-10 42-75207/*Rozzie Geth*/ *"BOCHE BUSTER"* of Lt Fred Christensen, 62nd FS/56th FG, Halesworth, March 1944

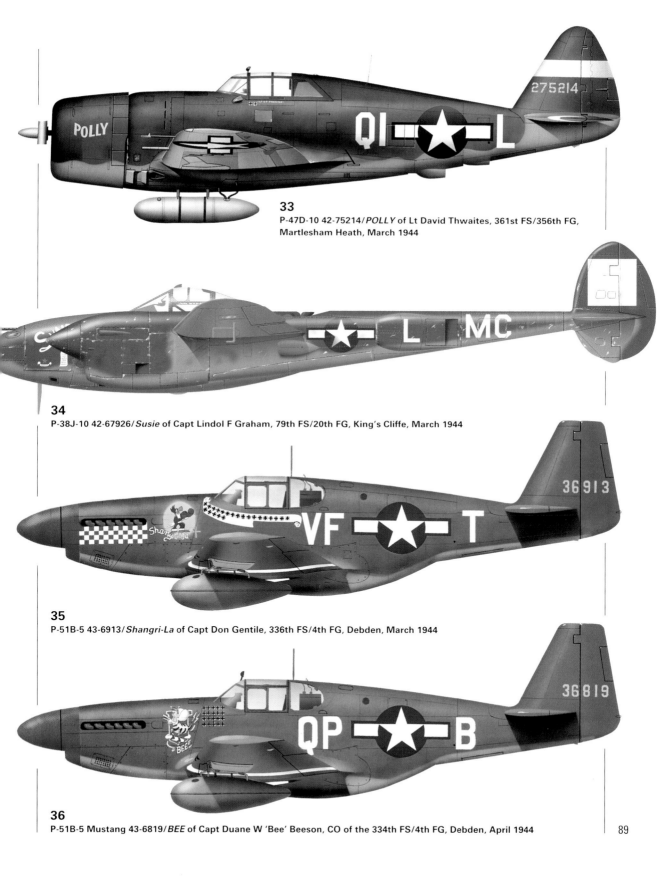

**33**
P-47D-10 42-75214/*POLLY* of Lt David Thwaites, 361st FS/356th FG,
Martlesham Heath, March 1944

**34**
P-38J-10 42-67926/*Susie* of Capt Lindol F Graham, 79th FS/20th FG, King's Cliffe, March 1944

**35**
P-51B-5 43-6913/*Shangri-La* of Capt Don Gentile, 336th FS/4th FG, Debden, March 1944

**36**
P-51B-5 Mustang 43-6819/*BEE* of Capt Duane W 'Bee' Beeson, CO of the 334th FS/4th FG, Debden, April 1944

**37**
P-47D-10 42-75068 of Lt Raymond Wetmore, 370th FS/359th FG, East Wretham, April 1944

**38**
P-47D-21 42-25512/*Penrod and Sam* of Capt Robert Johnson, 62nd FS/56th FG, Boxted, May 1944

**39**
P-38J-15 43-104308/*'Gentle Annie'* of Col Harold J Rau, CO of the 20th FG, King's Cliffe, April 1944

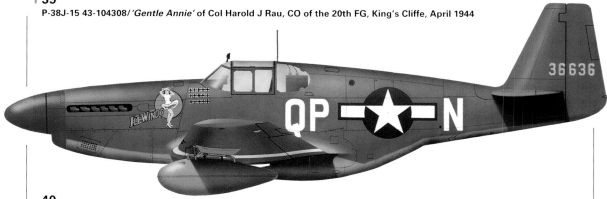

**40**
P-51B-5 43-6636/*ILL WIND?* of 1Lt Nicholas 'Cowboy' Megura, 334th FS/4th FG, Debden, April 1944

**41**
P-51B-10 43-7172/*Thunder Bird* of 1Lt Ted Lines, 335th FS/4th FG, Debden, April 1944

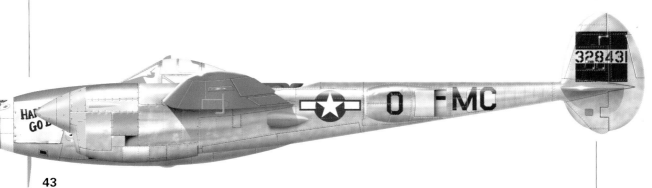

**42**
P-51B-5 43-6928/*OLE-II* of Capt William 'Billy' Hovde, 358th FS/355th FG, Steeple Morden, April 1944

**43**
P-38J-15 43-28431/*HAPPY JACK'S GO BUGGY* of Capt Jack M Ilfrey, 79th FS/20th FG, King's Cliffe, May 1944

**44**
P-47D-22 42-26044/*Silver Lady* of Maj Leslie Smith, 61st FS/56th FG, Boxted, May 1944

**45**
P-38J (serial unknown) *Janet* of Capt Thomas A White, 338th FS/55th FG, Wormingford, May 1944

**46**
P-51B-15 42-106924/*Salem Representative* of 2Lt Ralph 'Kid' Hofer, 334th FS/4th FG, Debden, May 1944

**47**
P-51B-10 42-106449/*Princess ELIZABETH* of 1Lt William 'Bill' Whisner, 487th FS/352nd FG, Bodney, May 1944

**48**
P-51B-10 42-106448/*THE HUN HUNTER FROM TEXAS* of 1Lt Henry 'Baby' Brown, 354th FS/355th FG, Steeple Morden, May 1944

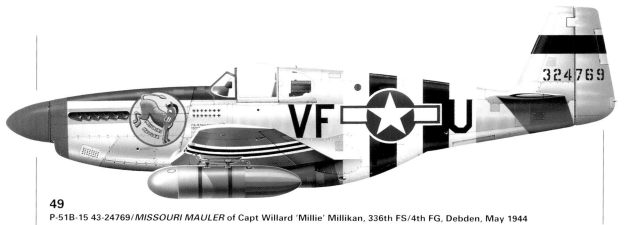

**49**
P-51B-15 43-24769/*MISSOURI MAULER* of Capt Willard 'Millie' Millikan, 336th FS/4th FG, Debden, May 1944

**50**
P-38J-10 42-68008/*Touché* of Lt Col James Herren, CO of the 434th FS/479th FG, Wattisham, June 1944

**51**
P-51B-15 43-24824/*OLD CROW* of Capt Clarence 'Bud' Anderson, 362nd FS/357th FG, Leiston, June 1944

**52**
P-51B-5 43-6933/*SPEEDBALL ALICE* of
1Lt Donald Bochkay, 363rd FS/357th FG, Leiston, June 1944

**1**
Lt Col Dave Schilling, Deputy CO of the 56th FG at Halesworth in March 1944

**2**
Col 'Hub' Zemke, CO of the 56th FG at Halesworth in December 1943

**3**
Lt Robert Johnson of the 61st FS/56th FG at Halesworth in October 1943

**4**
Maj Gerry Johnson of the
360th FS/356th FG at Martlesham
Heath in January 1944

**5**
Capt 'Gabby' Gabreski, CO of the
61st FS/56th FG at Horsham St Faith
in June 1943

**6**
Lt Col Eugene Roberts, Deputy CO of
the 78th FG at Duxford in October
1943

**7**
Lt James Morris of the 77th FS/20th FG at King's Cliffe in February 1944

**8**
Capt Lindol 'Lindy' Graham of the 79th FS/20th FG at King's Cliffe in September 1943

5. My wingman stays as close to me as possible while manoeuvring. When straight and level, he moves out to one side, line abreast, about one-half mile.

6. I would hit the deck when heavily outnumbered, or on one engine and under attack by enemy aircraft.

### OFFENSIVE

1. The wingman moves out to the side so we can protect each other's tail. He only attacks an enemy aircraft working on me if directed by me to attack another aircraft. Then I cover him. We do not attack the same aeroplane under any circumstances.

2. The enemy will try turning with us and then invariably half rolls. We spiral after him as we cannot follow him in a prolonged dive due to buffeting in the P-38, although we can initially out-dive him.

3. The force with the greatest altitude does the attacking. We attack any numbers when we have altitude. We zoom back up unless we are able to follow him when he half rolls or turns. We always try to get on his tail and get a minimum deflection shot. We always leave a portion of the force for top cover.

4. It is inadvisable to attack the enemy when he has top cover above us and superior numbers also. Unless we can attack the top cover first, we try to avoid combat. Generally, he attacks anyway, but we can't beat off his attack, then his top cover is generally gone, so it winds up into a free-for-all.

5. To avoid overshooting, dive below him and pull up after him to kill speed. Throw down combat flaps and retard throttles. We stay until buffeting starts.

6. Wingman should be out to the side at least one-quarter mile.

7. I try to fire in line dead astern, but will fire at any deflection if range is under 500 yards.

8. To break off combat, out-climb him if under 20,000 ft. Out-turn him and head for some help. We can outrun him up to 25,000 ft with an even start.

## Formation Combat Tactics

### GENERAL

1. If the R/V is reached with full 16-ship squadrons, stack one squadron on each side of the leading half of the bomber division, with the leading squadron ten miles in front of the leading wing. Squadrons are opened up to about ten miles between extreme aircraft, always trying to maintain flights line abreast. If squadrons have 12 or less aircraft, we 'S' over the top of the leading half of the bomb division in columns of squadrons, flights line abreast.

2. Control is delegated to squadrons when better than three to four miles apart. Squadrons control flights until flights attack.

3. Flights can call out an attack and request cover. Squadron leader gives decision to permit attack. Permission to attack is generally understood as affirmative.

4. Flight leader always starts attack, but many times he tells element leader to do so if element leader is in a better position after a few turns, etc. Wingmen don't attack except rarely when they might be in the best position. Whoever attacks is always covered by the other half of the flight or element.

5. After taking position with the bombers, from one-half to one mile should be the distance between any two units, whether it be individuals, elements, flights, or sections.

6. Flights fly fairly tight if there is more than one flight. Always half of the force is at least one-half mile from the other half.

7. Through radio transmission and giving position with respect to the bomber formation, it is generally quite easy for flights to join up with the squadron after combat.

8. I believe 12 or more ships can range anywhere within sight of the

**Well-worn Olive Drab and Neutral Gray P-38Js of the 383rd FS/364th FG rendezvous with the bombers over a typically cloudy East Anglia in the late spring of 1944. Based at Honington from February 1944 through to war's end, the 383rd marked its Lightnings both with the code 'N2' and a large white circle – the latter unfortunately obscuring the serial number. The factory construction number is, however, still carried on the nose of the P-38 closest to the camera (*via Michael O'Leary*)**

bombers. So long as the bombers can be seen, you can request aid by giving position from bombers. A group should be the minimum for despatch into enemy territory, and they should always be within sight of each other or a good reference point visible to all.

**DEFENSIVE**

1. Our standard line abreast formation is always in position to beat off any attack.

2. A small enemy aircraft force will be engaged by a portion of our force so the rest may continue on their mission. If the enemy force is large and we are defensive, it will wind up into a free-for-all. We definitely try to keep our force within supporting distances through radio transmission.

3. The attack has to be determined and prolonged to force us to drop tanks. This aeroplane handles very well with belly tanks.

4. Almost all enemy attacks are still from dead astern and start from above. Occasionally a head-on pass is made, but we can shoot as well as he, and our firepower is superior.

5. In the briefing I tell the pilots all I know about power settings, rate of climb, courses, desired position of squadrons, tactics for today (usually depends on bomber force, our force and other fighters with us).

6. I would never order a formation to hit the deck if there were two or more aircraft until we were over water.

**OFFENSIVE**

1. I delegate an attack to the flight in the best position.

2. I send twice the number of the enemy for two reasons – we are operating over their territory and need superior numbers to guard against a trap, and he will always split up so we will never have to break down into less than two aircraft working together.

3. When the enemy has the advantage of position we let him attack, turn into him, keep going on with our mission or pursue him if our mission is to do so.

4. The enemy will try to dive away from P-38s. We follow him to the deck if we think we can catch him.

5. We always try to engage before he attacks the bombers.

6. We always approach the bombers from up sun side. Clouds cannot be used offensively as it is too difficult to keep the fighters together on instruments. Thin high clouds above the bombers can be used as a screen between you and the bombers. I do not think the bombers can screen fighters due to our having to 'S'.

7. Our policy of trying to keep a flight together (minimum) does not hinder attack.

8. Flight leaders always call a bounce. They can attack without permission, but I cannot remember any instance when permission was not given and further information about cover was also given.

### Mark Everett Hubbard

Born on 17 August 1913 in Wisconsin, Mark Hubbard attended the University of Minnesota before joining the Army as a flying cadet. Commissioned on 11 May 1940, he was an experienced fighter pilot by the time America entered World War 2. Sent to North Africa as the commander of the 59th FS/33rd FG, Hubbard led his unit, and their P-40s, on a daring take-off from the USS *Chataga* off Casablanca on 10 November 1942 as part of the Allied invasion of North Africa.

Mark Hubbard enjoyed all of his success with the Lightning on 18 March 1944. Flying P-38J-10 42-67708, he led the 20th FG on a bomber escort mission deep into Germany – VIII Fighter Command units protected in excess of 700 B-17s and B-24s on this day. Intercepting a large force of Bf 109s over Memmingen, the 20th FG was embroiled in a ferocious fight that saw Hubbard down two fighters himself, share in the destruction of a third and claim a fourth as a probable. Still more aircraft continued to attack the bombers despite the best efforts of the escorts, and Hubbard was duly downed by a Bf 109 over Augsburg. He bailed out and was made a PoW (*20th FG Association*)

Hubbard began his string of victories on 15 January 1943 when he shot down two Ju 88s. He transferred to the P-38-equipped 20th FG at King's Cliffe, in England, in February 1944, and was given command of the group on 3 March 1944. Hubbard's period in charge was to last just 15 days, however, for on 18 March he was shot down by a Bf 109 after claiming two (and one shared) Messerschmitt fighters in a fierce dogfight near Augsburg – on a positive note, he achieved 'acedom' during this eventful mission. Parachuting from his stricken aircraft, Hubbard was captured and interned in *Stalag Luft I* in the German city of Barth.

Following repatriation, he remained in the USAF and retired as a full colonel in October 1963. Hubbard then moved to Canada and established his own business, which provided consulting services to Northrop Aircraft Corporation. He died in August 1984.

Mark Hubbard was credited with 6.5 confirmed victories and one probable.

# Maj Herbert E Johnson Jr
## Commanding Officer
### 77th FS/20th FG

The initiation of pilots into combat flying is something like teaching a boxer how to fight – you can tell him over and over everything you know, but if he does not actually *practice* what he hears when he gets in the ring, your teaching is of no avail. However, since it is impossible to ride with a fighter pilot, the next best method is incessant and continual lecturing and 'bull sessions'. I might point out that this P-38 we are flying requires a far greater knowledge of its mechanical and aerodynamic characteristics on the part of the pilot than is normally required to fly fighters.

We can definitely turn inside any German aircraft. This particular advantage is especially valuable when escorting bombers on deep penetrations when we are actually in a defensive position. When being attacked, say from above and behind, the timing of the break (turn into attack) is the key to success. If the flight is line astern, the number four and three men may have to break first followed by the flight leader and wingman. Breaking too soon lets the Hun cut across the turn. Naturally, breaking too late would be disastrous. It is possible to reverse the turn after breaking into an attack and end up on the Hun's tail if he's not too sharp.

Preferably, a wingman should fly close enough so he can act with his leader. In attacking enemy aircraft it is desirable to have the wingmen flare out to the side, as well as the second element. In making an attack, one naturally will take advantage of any cloud available, or the sun if possible. However, the main idea is to attack without hesitation to achieve the greatest element of surprise. The combat flap can be used to good advantage to avoid overshooting. Personally, I find deflection shooting to be a matter of judgement by eye, which is probably of no value to others. I fire when I judge myself to be within 200-150 yards on a closing attack, using deflection as I judge by eye with partial aid of the ring

Hailing from Los Angeles, Maj Herbert E Johnson led the 77th FS/20th FG from November 1943 through to March 1944, when he became Deputy CO of the group. Awarded a Distinguished Flying Cross and the Air Medal with three Oak Leaf Clusters during his time in the ETO, Johnson was also credited with 3.5 victories by the end of his tour (*via Michael O'Leary*)

One of the USAAF's great fighter aces, Maj J D 'Whispering John' Landers had already 'made ace' on P-40Es in the Pacific as long ago as Boxing Day 1942 when he joined the 38th FS/55th FG in April 1944. He added a further four kills (a Bf 109G on 25 June and three Me 410s on 7 July) and a damaged (another Bf 109G) to his tally whilst flying the P-38J-15, rising to command the 38th FS in early July 1944. Landers' final 4.5 kills were scored with the P-51D whilst on his third combat tour (as CO of the 78th FG) in March 1945 (*via John Stanaway*)

Although early P-38 operations were plagued by the initial unsuitability of the big Lockheed fighter to the high altitude operations that characterised the ETO, morale amongst pilots in VIII Fighter Command remained high. These 338th FS/55th FG pilots watch a colleague demonstrate his rather unorthodox method for combating one of the Lightning's most notorious (and enduring) features in north-west Europe – the icy cold cockpit temperature. Men from this group, based at Nuthampstead, flew the first Eighth Air Force aircraft over Berlin, on 3 March 1944 (*via John Stanaway*)

Capt Chet Patterson of the 338th FS/55th FG was a daring and cunning flight leader who claimed four German aircraft destroyed before being posted home on rotation, having just failed to secure that elusive fifth kill. He was one of the first pilots in the ETO to appreciate the positive fighting points of the P-38 – firepower, range and manoeuvrability (*via John Stanaway*)

P-38J-10 42-67757 of the 55th FG's 38th FS was the subject of an extensive recognition photo-shoot soon after the fighter's arrival in the UK at the end of 1943. The results of the flight were widely circulated throughout Allied air and ground forces in order to familiarise 'the troops' (particularly bomber gunners and anti-aircraft battery crews) with the shape of the Lightning from all possible angles (*via John Stanaway*)

P-38Js of the 38th FS/55th FG are seen on a bomber escort mission during May 1944. This month saw Lightnings flying both escort and ground attack missions in preparation for D-Day. Late spring 1944 was also a period of transition for fighters in the ETO, as new aircraft began to be taken on strength in a natural metal finish, rather the traditional olive drab and grey (*via John Stanaway*)

sight. In attacking twin-engined aircraft I like to approach from above, diving down to slightly below when closing in. In these attacks, if proper top cover is available I like to see a wingman space his approach so as to fire also. Always break away level or down.

I do not recommend hitting the deck if altitude can be maintained, unless you become separated completely, and then be damn sure of

your approximate whereabouts. If jumped on the deck, the best evasive manoeuvre is a tight level turn. Due to the beautiful stall characteristics of the P-38, you can turn much tighter than any German craft without the danger of spinning in.

Our best formation going out to the rendezvous has proved to be the line abreast. This is carried out by flights abreast, but men within the flights fly at a comfortable angle. The in-sun squadron will fly below the lead squadron and slightly behind, and the down-sun squadron is above and slightly back so as to see the leader down through the engine and cockpit. A 500-ft difference in elevation of squadrons is suf-ficient. The big advantage of this formation is the cross cover, which practically eliminates being bounced without first seeing the enemy.

The important point involved is not to have any stragglers. Keep everyone well up so there is *no* tail end Charlie. A peculiar point in fighting the Hun is that he seems to know, or sense, when you see him, even if above (he is generally above you), and hesitates to attack aggressively in this event. As sure as this, he also seems to know how to bounce when you don't see him.

Several types of cover can be employed with the bombers. If the squadrons consist of 16 ships or more, one can be assigned to cover a whole box or two of bombers. If the group numbers around 32 or less, it is best to work as a group. In no case will a section (eight ships) split unless a flight becomes a general melee and it is impossible to maintain contact. Sections work best by flying the two flights abreast across the bombers at 45 or 60 degrees to line of flight of bombers. The turn away from the sun should be fast.

If the bombers are comparatively high (27,000 to 29,000 ft) it is advisable to work the squadrons on either side and one on top – this is old practice in this theatre. Generally, the group leader will determine the disposition of the squadrons at time of rendezvous depending on the size of force to be covered, altitude of highest and lowest boxes, and type of formation the bombers are flying.

Naturally, the ideal situation is to maintain close co-operation between all units, squadrons, sections, flights and elements, but the

**P-38H-5 42-67057 of the 338th FS/ 55th FG was photographed departing Nuthampstead on one of the group's very first operational missions in October 1943. Note the short-lived red surround to the national insignia (*via Michael O'Leary*)**

ability to do this depends on the situation. It generally becomes necessary to break down to sections and flights in order to break up attacks on the bombers, which may occur at any point or time. A squadron should definitely remain intact, or at least in the same vicinity for mutual support and protection. We have found that even one flight remaining as top cover is a tremendous help, and acts as a strong deterrent to the Hun in attacking our lower people, or those engaged in attacking enemy aircraft.

In a squadron or section the flights fly line abreast, but the men in the flights will fly about on a 45-degree angle. If a flight is alone, then the element comes up abreast. When a fight breaks a squadron up into flights, they can best rejoin by taking up a common heading (called out over the radio transmitter by leader), or if with bombers, rejoin on them.

The formation should definitely not be too tight, but in any case the distance should be taken laterally and not longitudinally to line of flight – 50 yards between leader and wingman, 100 yards between elements, 400 yards between flights and 800 yards between squadrons are rough figures. On deep penetration the fighter group is obviously somewhat in a defensive position due to the necessity to conserve gasoline. However, when an advantage exists to 'bounce' the Hun on his way up, it should be taken.

I usually try to hold belly tanks until empty or actually engaged. The only way to give effective support to bombers is to conserve all gas possible on the way in.

I don't think the Hun has worked out anything new in 'tricks' or tactics other than trying to imitate our formations. Due to the ease of recognising the P-38 as an 'enemy', and the considerable confusion in segregating the single-engined friendly and enemy, we are at a slight disadvantage in making identifications. This calls for better recognition skills and quicker judgement on our part.

Briefing procedure could fill several pages, but I do feel it necessary to go into the disposition of squadrons and flights in detail. The more you have understood before climbing into the cockpit, the easier it is to join up and carry out the mission in general.

In making attacks on enemy aircraft, the flight or element best able to attack without delay will do so. Generally, this will be the flight which calls in the bandit. Considerable help is given by calling out the direction you are bouncing in, and whether low or level. It helps keep the outfit together.

I really believe that in making the actual attack, more instinct enters in than by following a given procedure. If an outfit can fly good formation at ease and look around plenty, there should be no trouble. It's really impossible to lay down any set rules for bouncing. The important point is to always cover a bounce, and not fall for the Hun's old sucker play.

(OFFICIAL NOTE – it might be wise to reflect that the hun would not be continuing his 'old sucker play' – i.e. exposing a low flight to our attack with a superior force, high and hidden in sun or cloud, ready to bounce if we do – unless he was still having some success with it.)

# CAPT MAURICE R MCLARY
# 55th FS/20th FG

On one encounter, my squadron was returning from an escort mission when we were engaged by 14 long-nosed Fw 190s. Apparently, they had been scrambled and vectored to us because they came in from six o'clock and were climbing. We were then at 12,000-13,000 ft.

On first impression, we thought we'd outrun them since our mission was completed and we were only a few miles from the coast. We still had our belly tanks, and before we could drop them and 'pour on the coal', four of the enemy aircraft, flying line abreast, started firing at our last man. I broke quickly and started to attack four (one flight of enemy aircraft) head-on. Two of them half-rolled and hit the deck, but the other two broke away from me and started climbing. I followed them into a steep climbing turn to the left, closing in fast. I destroyed the No 2 man and damaged the leader.

From this encounter, I would say that anyone flying a P-38 should have no fear of any enemy aircraft – even dogfighting a single-engined fighter at a decent altitude. I consider anything below 20,000 ft a decent altitude for a P-38.

On the encounters I've had with the enemy's twin-engined aircraft, I have found that they can turn much shorter than I had anticipated. I've also had trouble in staying behind them – the tendency being to over-run them. They usually try to out-turn you and in so doing, put their tail gunner in a good position. I learned this the hard way – by having an engine shot out by an Me 110 tail gunner.

I want my wingman to stay with me at *all* times. I never hit the deck if I can get out any other way.

As for shooting, range seems to be the hardest thing to estimate correctly. Personally, I close in to that point where I feel I am about 300 yards from the target, then I hold my fire until I close to one-half that distance. This way I'm always sure of being within range.

The 20th FG's Capt Maurice McLary was officially credited with three destroyed and three damaged during his tour of the ETO. When he claimed his first kill on 24 January 1944, he had the dubious distinction of being 'stung' by the rear gunner of the Bf 110 that he eventually shot down. McLary's P-38 was hit by return fire in the fuel transfer system, and he was forced to fly back to his King's Cliffe base with two inches of petrol sloshing around in the bottom of the cockpit! (*20th FG Association*)

P-38J-10 42-67717 was the personal mount of leading Eighth Air Force P-38 ace James 'Slick' Morris of the 20th FG's 77th FS (*via Bill Hess*)

When leading a squadron, I despatch a full section to take the bounce if I have a 16-ship squadron behind me. The other section remains as cover. Of course, every situation calls for different tactics, but I feel that the part of the squadron in the best position to take the bounce should do it, rather than the section which spots the enemy.

The best way to attack a twin-engined aircraft is to close at high speed, opening fire at 700 to 800 yards, then break away level to come back for another pass.

## CAPT MERLE B NICHOLS 79th FS/20th FG

A head-on attack calls for quick recognition and a light trigger finger.

After making a break, if we can make the enemy aircraft commit himself by turning with us or doing anything but a split-S, we can usually be on the offensive in a matter of seconds.

If over enemy territory, either alone or with a small number (four or less), you can, as a rule, always expect an attack to be from the sun. If you climb up sun and can watch the enemy aircraft behind you, it is very difficult for him to press his attack home. When he breaks off because of this, a U-turn will put you on him.

If crippled or on one engine, a few minutes of instruments in the clouds to get away from immediate vicinity of the bombers, or off of the bomber's track, will help to avoid being hit. In using the clouds for protection *never* fly just under them. It is best to fly above them and drop down if necessary.

If attacked by superior numbers, a flight of four should do a Lufberry. If in a section of eight, then carry out two opposite direction Lufberrys, one above the other about 500 to 800 ft.

When on the deck, if both engines are running okay – full RPM and maximum manifold pressure – the Hun does not have an aircraft that can catch us. The deck is not the place to be caught. A 30-degree change in direction every few minutes will keep enemy aircraft from being vectored to you.

If I am being attacked, my wingman should break with me. If he is being attacked, he should break, and I will follow him.

Merle Nicholls poses with the 79th FS's armaments officer, Lt Charles Smith, at King's Cliffe in early 1944. Note the 'pin-up' slotted into the pilot's thigh map pocket. Nicholls, who later commanded the 77th FS from mid-December 1944 to war's end, was credited with three kills and two damaged during his time in the ETO. In a strange twist of fate, he scored his first and final victories on the same date, but a full year to the day apart – 14 January 1944 and 1945! (*20th FG Association*)

Single-engined enemy aircraft, as a rule, split-S to evade attack. The thing to do is surprise him, get him in close range and destroy him before he has a chance to get away.

Superior enemy numbers make little difference if you have the advantage, plenty of gasoline and can keep a part of your number above the attack for cover. The Hun does not like to be attacked and will run at every opportunity and try to get home so he can come back at another time when *he* has the advantage.

It is inadvisable to attack if coming home low on gasoline, or with a cripple in the flight. Never attack twin-engined enemy aircraft until you have made certain they don't have an escort sitting on top. Attack only when conditions are favourable. An even trade of aircraft is not a good show.

Avoid overshooting by not getting up too much speed in diving down. Come in from high altitude, 'S'ing' down and getting in position with a maximum of 100 mph greater air speed than the enemy aircraft has. Use combat flaps if necessary.

My shooting methods have one aim – *dead astern at 50 ft*. I break off attack with a sharp, steep chandelle towards the group or bombers.

Never less than eight aircraft should work together, two flights of four each. Each squadron should stay together as much as possible, and the squadron should be in the near vicinity so if one bites off more than he can chew he can receive help from the other two.

P-38J-10 42-67451 was flown by a Capt Schultz of the 20th FG's 79th FS during the spring and early summer of 1944. Note the traditional mission markers of VIII Fighter Command (*via Bill Hess*)

The wingman has as many guns as the flight leader, but he is there to offer protection, and should use good, sound judgement.

Formation with the bombers is line abreast within the flight, and the two flights line abreast. Again one half-mile apart or so, it is possible to turn inside with about one third the distance to spare.

Always form up after combat on a particular box of bombers at a given altitude.

Our formations are loose enough as we fly them to provide plenty of flexibility.

When enemy aircraft are in position to attack, we wait until they get to our altitude, then start the break at the proper time. Make sure that all members of the flight understand the situation so the break does not come as a complete surprise to any one member.

We don't drop our belly tanks until we are ready to. We can take a bounce with them on.

The enemy has recently been putting out a patrol across our fighter and bomber tracks to pick up cripples on their way home (50 to 100 miles inland). A good counter measure would be to put a group of our own there and get the cripples back.

I have had the occasion to use 'hit the deck' only once, and that was when we were separated from our group and section, and too many enemy aircraft were around and were some 15,000 ft below the bombers. We stayed there for 30 minutes, then climbed back up line abreast and came out that way. Remember to always keep the speed well up while climbing. It works. We came home and lived to fight another day.

Whoever is in the best position makes the bounce. No one in the US Army Air Corps gives a damn who gets credit for the victory, just so the Hun is destroyed. When one flight makes a bounce the other flight should remain as top cover, and let nothing draw them away except when the flight doing the bouncing is being hit. The bouncing flight should always be well informed by radio transmission just what the situation is so they can proceed with what they are doing and feel secure that they are protected.

My theory is *no* less than eight aeroplanes working together as a team – one flight for cover and the other for attack – should be sent down to make a bounce.

When the enemy has the advantage of position and altitude, wait them out and make them commit themselves. Don't climb for them; let them come down. If you go to 30,000 they go to 35,000, etc. We, with our type of aircraft, like them below 25,000 and, if possible, at 20,000.

If the aeroplanes are heading away from our course home, we will pursue them a lot less than otherwise. At the most I would say 15 miles away from the group.

In the ETO, or any theatre of war, the individual flight leader's initiative, and how they co-operate and work together, is the deciding factor in how well a group shows up in combat. A too eager flight leader will lose more wingmen, and sooner or later himself, and get less victories than one who attacks at the opportune time, and tries to make certain that the attack is going to be a profitable one.

Capt Lindol Graham stands with his crew chief S/Sgt Morris in front of their P-38J-10 42-67497 soon after the future Lightning ace had claimed three Fw 190s in a single mission on 29 January 1944. Graham named each of his P-38s *Susie*, and they usually flew with the code letters 'MC-L' applied to the fighter's twin booms. This particular aircraft was paid for by Lockheed employees, and was dedicated to a former worker who had been killed in action (*via John Stanaway*)

# P-51 MUSTANG PILOTS

## CAPT D W BEESON
## 334th FS/4th FG

I received your letter some time ago and am sorry for waiting so long to answer. It's pretty hard to give a reply on the questions you ask about tactics in air fighting, so I'll just try to give a few personal ideas, and if this isn't too late you might be able to fit one or two of them in somewhere.

Probably the best thing to say on tactics is that they do alter, and depend entirely on each situation as it exists at the moment. The only rules that can be laid out for actual combat are pretty general, and it just takes plain common sense to apply them at the right time.

I think that the most important one thing to a fighter pilot is speed! The faster an aircraft is moving when he spots an enemy aircraft, the sooner he will be able to take the bounce and get to the Hun. And it's harder for him to bounce you if you are going fast. Of course, keeping a high speed in formations is very hard because the formation falls apart, and also because of trying to save gas. But it is an important thing for a pilot to remember when he gets separated from his group, or when split up into small units. Also, when actually bouncing a Hun it is good to have as much speed as possible. The aircraft that has speed has the advantage on the one that hasn't. He has the initiative because speed can always be converted into altitude.

The problem of overshooting a Hun comes up quite often in both the P-47 and the P-51 because of the very high overtaking speed they pick up in the dive. And sometimes pilots report after a combat that they couldn't get the

Duane 'Bee' Beeson became the 4th FG's first ace when he downed two Bf 109s in this very aircraft (P-47D-1 42-7890) on 8 October 1943. Indeed, all 12 of his Thunderbolt kills were achieved in this Republic fighter, which he christened *BOISE BEE* after his home town. This official USAAF photo of Beeson and one of his dedicated groundcrew was taken at Debden between 14 and 29 January 1944 (*via Roger Freeman*)

Louis H 'Red Dog' Norley had the unique distinction of serving with all three squadrons within the 4th FG during his two tours in the ETO. He claimed 7.333 kills with the 336th FS (flying P-47s and then P-51s) during the course of his first tour, two more victories whilst serving with the 335th FS at the start of his second spell in the frontline, and then a further pair (although he was only officially credited with one victory) following his move to the 334th FS in January 1945. Norley also commanded both the 334th and 335th FSs at various times between late August 1944 and late September 1945 (*via Dick Martin*)

Hun they were attacking because they 'overshot him'. And the question is asked, 'How do you avoid overshooting?'

My own idea is that overshooting is a very good thing. Speed is good and should never be lost. When you keep a high speed up you can be sure of closing into range before opening fire, and the closer you get, the better chance you have of hitting him. Also, another good point to remember is that when you are bouncing a Hun you are on the offensive and have the advantage. But things happen in split seconds up there,

**Above**
One of the most flamboyant characters to fly with VIII Fighter Command was Ralph 'Kid' Hofer, who joined the Royal Canadian Air Force prior to America's entry into the war. He was amongst the first 4th FG pilots to 'make ace' with the Mustang in the ETO, scoring six of his eventual fifteen kills in this P-51B-15 (42-106924), which he named *Salem Representative* in honour of his home town in Missouri. He is seen here with the 334th FS's orphan dog, Duke, which adopted Hofer. This official USAAF photograph was taken at Debden on 14 May 1944 (*via Dick Martin*)

**Above right**
The 'Kid' holds court outside the 334th Operations Hut at Debden. He is explaining his latest victory whilst simultaneously smoking his first cigarette following the completion of yet another long bomber escort mission to Germany. Note his non-regulation long hair and lucky college football jersey, which he religiously wore on every sortie (*via Dick Martin*)

**Bottom right**
One of Hofer's contemporaries in the 334th FS was Nicholas 'Cowboy' Megura who, like the 'Kid', had been trained by the Canadians. Another to enjoy early success with the Mustang, Megura was credited with 11.833 kills and six damaged between 4 March and 22 May 1944 (*via Bill Hess*)

and you don't know what might happen, so that you will suddenly find the same Hun, or one of his friends, back on your tail shooting at you. And if you are still going faster than he is, it is easy to pull back on the stick and zoom up above him, where you are ready to attack again.

Never give the Hun an even break. If you have any advantage on him, keep it and use it. So, when attacking, I would say plan to

An early advocate for the Merlin-engined Mustang was Don Blakeslee, who argued forcefully with senior USAAF officers for the allocation of the North American fighter to the strategic Eighth Air Force rather than the tactical Ninth. Having heard great things about the re-engined fighter's altitude performance and range from his contacts in the North American flight test team back in California, Blakeslee got himself temporarily seconded to the Ninth Air Force's 354th FG in December 1943. This unit was the first to fly the P-51B in the ETO, and after just a few short weeks in combat with the aircraft, Blakeslee was convinced that it was clearly the best American fighter in-theatre. The first examples duly arrived with the 4th FG in February 1944, and Blakeslee (who was now CO of the group) went on to claim eight of his 14.5 kills with the Mustang. This photograph shows him sat in his assigned P-51B-5 43-6437, which he kept devoid of both nose-art and kill markings. Note both its weathered appearance and highly-prized 'blown' Malcolm canopy hood (via Dick Martin)

When photographed in March 1945 following its 'in-the-field' conversion into the 4th FG's first two-seat Mustang, this aircraft had already completed a long tour in the frontline with the 335th FS. Boasting a unique code to denote its dual capacity, the former fighter was used by the group's 'Clobber College' Operational Training Unit (via Dick Martin)

The chief architect in the modification of P-51B 43-12193 into a 'two-holer' was the 335th FS's senior technical inspector, T/Sgt 'Woody' Jensen, who is seen here sat in the aircraft's front cockpit. Crouching on the wing is the 4th FG's engineering officer, Capt Grunow – the third individual in this photo remains unidentified. Note how the glazing for the Mustang is provided by two standard P-51B canopies (*via Dick Martin*)

Pilots from the 334th FS enjoy hot coffee and doughnuts at their dispersal courtesy of a GI-booted American Red Cross volunteer in the spring of 1944 (*via Dick Martin*)

Yet another early P-51 ace, Maj George 'Carp' Carpenter had claimed 13.833 kills, one probable and eight damaged by the time he was shot down in action on 18 April 1944 and captured – he had downed two fighters in the minutes prior to his demise. Canadian trained, Carpenter led the 335th FS from 5 February 1944 until made a PoW (*via Tom Ivie*)

overshoot him if possible, and hold fire until within range, then shoot and clobber him down to the last instant before breaking away. It's sorta' like sneaking up behind and hitting him with a baseball bat. When this is done, a pilot will have to be careful not to ram the other aircraft on the breakaway. As he overshoots and pulls up sharply above the Hun, he can take a quick look around to clear his tail, and then concentrate on his Hun again, making as many passes and overshoots as necessary to finish him off.

When the enemy is taking violent evasive action it is hard to get a good shot at him if you are going too fast, so speed can be cut down a little just as long as you are still going faster than he is. An attack of this kind prevents the combat turning into a dogfight with both aircraft at the same speed, each fighting for the advantage. If the Hun sees you coming he can turn into you and meet you semi-head on, but you can still zoom back up and come down on him again. He can't keep turning circles all day; sooner or later he must break for the deck and when he does this, he's had it.

Maj Pierce W McKennon belts out a tune in the 4th FG's bar in August 1944. McKennon enrolled in the Army Reserve in 1941 but washed out of flight training. He then followed a well trodden path north to Canada, where he joined the RCAF and flew Spitfires as a sergeant pilot. McKennon duly transferred to the 335th FS/4th FG at Debden on 22 February 1943, and flew P-47s before going on to Mustangs. Made CO of the 335th FS at the start of his second tour in the ETO in August 1944, McKennon shared his last victory of the war on Christmas Day – his final tally was 11 aerial kills, 2.5 damaged and 9.68 ground kills. Injured by flak on 16 April 1945, he was immediately retired from combat. Having successfully evaded twice, and survived 26 months in the ETO, Pierce McKennon was killed on 18 June 1947 when the AT-6 in which he was flying as an instructor crashed near San Antonio, Texas (*via Michael O'Leary*)

On 11 April 1944 Supreme Allied Commander Gen Dwight Eisenhower visited Debden with high-ranking USAAF officers including Lt Gen James H Doolittle (Commander Eighth Air Force), Gen Carl Spaatz (Commander US Strategic Air Forces in Europe) and Bill Kepner. After seeing a mock briefing and combat film, Eisenhower awarded DSCs to both Don Blakeslee and then leading ETO ace, and 336th FS pilot, Capt Don Gentile (*via John Stanaway*)

Having completed a maintenance check flight, Capt Don Gentile extricates himself from the cockpit of P-51B-5 43-6913 on 30 March 1944. His crew chief, S/Sgt John Ferra, stands forward of the cockpit, anxiously awaiting his pilot's verdict on the work he and his team have carried out. This aircraft had been grounded with engine problems following Gentile's 18 March mission to Munich. However, it had not stopped him from adding five kills to his tally in the intervening 11 days in P-51B-5 43-6572. With 43-6913 still grounded come Gentile's 1 April mission to Ludwigshafen-Mannheim, the ace claimed his 18th kill in 43-6572 instead (*via John Stanaway*)

Aside from the red and white chequers on the nose and distinctive kill scroll beneath the cockpt, Gentile's 42-6913 also boasted a rendition of the 336th FS's official unit emblem and the nickname *Shangri-La*. Both pilot and aircraft were the subject of much Press attention in late March and early April 1944 as Gentile closed on Eddie Rickenbacker's almost mythical tally of 26 kills (*via John Stanaway*)

Aces High! Nine pilots from the 336th FG were credited with five or more kills during World War 2, and the four highest scorers are all seen in this posed group shot, taken in March 1944. At the extreme left is Johnny Godfrey, who claimed 16.333 kills, then comes Don Gentile with 21.833 (two of these victories were scored with the RAF). Next to him is Peter Lehmann, son of Herbert Lehmann, Director of the US Office of Foreign Relief and former Governor of New York. Lehmann junior was killed on 31 March when his P-51B spun in during a low-level mock dogfight near Duxford, his aircraft suffering a violent centre of gravity change when the fuel load in its 65-gallon upright tank suddenly shifted due to the pilot's aggressive manoeuvring. Next to Lehmann is James Goodson, who scored 14 kills, and Willard Millikan who claimed 13 (*via Dick Martin*)

Probably the biggest thing to a fighter pilot is being able to see things – not only to see them, but to interpret them. When he sees fighters too far away to recognise, he should have a fairly good idea whether they are friendly or not by the way they act – by the way they circle a bomber formation or by the way they act when near other fighters that are known to be friendly. This is something that comes pretty much with experience, but a thing that can be practised is just looking and recognising what you see.

The final thing that makes a pilot decide what to do is when he definitely recognises the other aircraft as enemy or friendly – and the farther away it is when he does recognise it, the better chance he'll have

to get it, or to avoid boobing if it is a friend.

When flying, it is good to be looking constantly, and you can't look behind too often. Don't look quickly all over the sky – scan it slowly, section by section. When you see something that looks strange, keep an eye on it till it can be identified. The man who gets a Hun is usually the one who has seen it first.

A lot is heard about the use of the sun. It is true that an aircraft attacking out of the sun is very hard to see, which means that, defensively speaking, a pilot should always keep a better look-out in that direction than any other – especially if the sun is anywhere near his own tail. But when bouncing a Hun the sun means very little. When you see a Hun, hit him as fast as possible with everything you have before he gets away. If you wait to position yourself in the sun, the Jerry may be out of reach when you're ready to go. Or someone else may have reached him first and finished him off.

These are some personal ideas, some of them right and others may be wrong. Anyway, I know that other fellows will have different ideas on the same subject, and it will be good to read them over to learn something new. Maybe when you have received all these letters you

Wearing his crumpled '50 mission crush' Class A cap, 1Lt John T Godfrey poses on the wing of his P-51B-5 (43-6765) in early April 1944. Usually flying as a dual scoring element with squadronmate Don Gentile, Godfrey had his Mustang identically marked with red and white chequers to aid in forming up when airborne. Their partnership was the most productive in the 4th FG, for on 8 March they claimed six Bf 109s, followed by three more on the 23rd of that month and 4.333 kills (three Fw 190s, a Bf 109 and 0.333 of a He 111) six days later (via John Stanaway)

John Godfrey reputedly had the 'sharpest' eyes in the 4th FG, which goes a long way to explaining his success in action in 1943-44. Aside from his aerial successes, he was also credited with the destruction of 12.666 aircraft on the ground. And like most VIII Fighter Command aces brought down in action, it was his passion for strafing that would prove his downfall. However, Godfrey was not hit by flak in his P-51D on 24 August 1944. Instead, his fighter was terminally damaged by machine gun fire from his wingman, Lt Melvin Dickey! Godfrey had destroyed four Ju 52s at an airfield at Nordhausen just prior to his untimely demise. He would see out the rest of the war as a PoW (via Dick Martin)

Left and below
Godfrey's squadronmate 'Millie' Millikan also fell victim to a P-51 over Germany, his aircraft being hit by a Mustang attempting to avoid a flak burst over Wittenburg on 30 May 1944. The 13-kill ace also became a PoW (via Dick Martin)

'Millie' Millikan was flying this P-51B-15 (43-24769) when he was hit by his wingman, 2Lt Sam Young Jr, in P-51B-15 43-24787. The *MISSOURI MAULER* was decorated with 14 crosses, although its pilot only actually claimed 13 kills (he had no probable or damaged credits). Millikan did, however, destroy two aircraft on the ground, so perhaps one of these has been added to his tally. He is seen strapped into the cockpit of the near new fighter at Debden sometime after 22 May 1944, when he had claimed his 13th aerial victory in this very machine. His crew chief, S/Sgt Neal Gallagher, is stood on the wing root (*both photos via Dick Martin*)

The 336th FS's 'Pappy' Groves guides a glycol line into the Mustang's engine whilst John Ferra works away on the stirrup pump. Early P-51Bs proved a mechanical nightmare for groundcrews at Debden, with aircraft suffering from rough-running engines, propellers throwing oil, chronic glycol leaks and auxiliary tank feed problems

can pick out pieces here and there that when put together will do us all a lot of good. Again – sorry for waiting so long – and I hope this isn't too late to do any good.

(OFFICIAL NOTE – Capt Beeson's significant point is speed of attack, closing so fast that he 'overshoots' the enemy after delivering a close-range blast of fire, 'sorta like sneaking up behind and hitting him with a baseball bat', as Beeson says. In this he is seconded by such outstanding fighters as Mahurin, Zemke, Schilling and others. Overshooting really means closing *too* fast, so fast the attacker has no chance to fire effectively at all.)

### Duane Willard 'Bee' Beeson

Born in Boise, Idaho, on 16 July 1921, 'Bee' Beeson eventually moved to California, where he worked as a hotel clerk. Deciding to leave this boring job behind, he joined the Royal Canadian Air Force on 23 June 1941, and was commissioned as a pilot officer

on 26 February 1942, being sent overseas shortly afterwards.

Once in England, Beeson firstly completed the five-month long Spitfire conversion course at RAF Usworth, just south of Newcastle-upon-Tyne, with No 55 Operational Training Unit, before being posted to No 71 'Eagle' Sqn at Debden, in Essex. He arrived on the unit on 5 September, and 24 days later he became a part of the US Army Air Force when No 71 Sqn was officially transferred to VIII Fighter Command control.

Now flying with the 4th FG, 2Lt Beeson was assigned to the 334th FS, which swapped its Spitfire VBs for P-47C Thunderbolts in early 1943.

He seemed to click with the Republic 'heavyweight', and scored his first victory on 19 May 1943 when he shot down a Bf 109 over Holland. From that point on his score rapidly rose, and he became the 4th FG's first ace on 8 October.

'Bee' Beeson was given command of the 334th FS on 15 March 1944 – by which time the unit had converted to P-51B Mustangs. On 5 April 1944, he was shot down by flak while strafing a German airfield at Brandenburg, near Berlin. Immediately taken prisoner, Beeson was released following the surrender of Germany. He elected to stay in the AAF postwar, and was promoted to lieutenant colonel on 24 October 1945.

However, a promising career was cut cruelly short when Duane 'Bee' Beeson died from a brain tumour on 13 February 1947, aged just 25.

Helmet off, mask unclipped and canopy cranked open, a visually weary Capt Duane 'Bee' Beeson slowly removes his gloves whilst mentally contemplating the six-hour mission that he has just completed. 'Bee' would soon be relating details of his flight to the 334th's 'IO' (Intelligence Officer) (*via Dick Martin*)

## MAJ GEORGE E PREDDY
## 487th FS/352nd FG

In reply to your letter I am writing down a few principles of operational flying. All of these facts or ideas are based upon experience in this theatre while flying the P-47 on fighter sweeps and escort missions.

Maj George Preddy quizzes fellow Bodney-based pilots on their successes in a recent mission in this heavily posed shot taken in the spring of 1944. Standing on the starboard wing of Preddy's P-51B-10 (42-106451) is Lt Malcolm C Pickering, who claimed four aerial and four strafing victories. At the extreme left of the photo is 1Lt Jack Thornell, who claimed 17.25 aerial kills to finish third in the group's ace listing – he was, however, the ranking ace in the 328th FS (*via Michael O'Leary*)

Like most of the great aces in the ETO, George Preddy was regularly photographed by both the USAAF and the Press (*352nd FG Association*)

The 352nd FG's second-ranking ace was John 'Whips' Meyer, who was George Preddy's CO in the 487th FS for most of the latter pilot's first tour in the ETO. P-51B-10 42-106471 was Meyer's first Mustang, and he claimed 5.5 victories with it in April-May 1944. The tally carried below the fighter's cockpit includes its pilot's kills in the P-47, as well as his ground strafing victories. This aircraft was lost on 7 June 1944 when it spun in over southern England after completing a strafing mission in support of the D-Day landings. Its pilot, Lt Clifford Garney, was killed in the crash (*via Sam Sox*)

To begin with, it is an old story that the pilot who doesn't get across the Channel will not see any action. One of the big problems in this theatre is weather, and since a good 50 per cent of our flying is done in instrument conditions, it is necessary that all pilots be proficient at instrument and close formation flying. The formation used going through an overcast is as follows. In the flight, the number two man flies on the leader's left wing with three and four on the right. In the squadron the flights fly line astern stacked down. The whole outfit is in very close, and if each man flies a steady position, it is possible to take 16 or 20 ships through an overcast. If visibility in the soup is very bad or turbulence exists, it becomes necessary to split the squadron into sections of two or more.

Christened *Frances B TOO!*, this P-51B-5 was the personal mount of Capt Ralph W 'Ham' Hamilton of the 487th FS. Like many of the aircraft within this unit, the fighter's personal markings were applied by Sgt Sam Perry. Within weeks of this shot being taken in May 1944, the spotless Mustang was adorned with full invasion stripes on the fuselage and wings. Hamilton's response to these markings was, 'Who in the Hell messed up my beautiful airplane'! George Preddy flew *Frances B TOO!* over the D-Day beaches on 8 June (*via Sam Sox*)

Lt John Bennett's P-51B-5 43-6506 had the distinction of being the sole sharkmouthed Mustang to serve with VIII Fighter Command. Assigned to the 497th FS in the early spring of 1944, its distinctive nose-art was applied just days after its arrival at Bodney (*via Sam Sox*)

When Lt Col John Meyer suggested to future 487th FS ace 1Lt Bill Whisner that he name his previously 'clean' P-51B-10 in honour of HRH Princess Elizabeth, he was less than enthusiastic about the idea. However, as this photo shows, his CO won the day! (*via Sam Sox*)

P-51B-15 43-24807 was flown by Capt 'Wally' Starck during the summer of 1944. He claimed two kills, one probable and one damaged in this aircraft during June-July, although this photograph was taken prior to him being issued with the fighter. On 27 November 1944 Starck was lost on what was supposed to be his 106th, and last, combat mission of his ETO tour. Having just claimed his seventh victory, his P-51D was struck by the tail section from the Bf 109 that he had just destroyed, forcing Starck to bail out into captivity (*via Michael O'Leary*)

Camouflaged and fully invasion striped Mustangs of the 486th and 487th FSs await a load of bombs before their next mission to Europe. Note how the individual aircraft letter was moved to the vertical and nose areas of some of the aircraft, having been obscured by the D-Day stripes (*via Michael O'Leary*)

1Lt Ed Heller of the 486th FS converses with his steel-helmeted groundcrew 'in the field' in front of his P-51B-5 43-6704. His impressive victory tally reflects a mix of aerial and strafing victories (*via Sam Sox*)

On the climb out, the flights and individual ships fly close formation, as this reduces throttle jockeying and saves gas. When we approach the enemy coast, everybody moves out into battle formation, – i.e. line abreast and five or six ships lengths apart for individual ships and line abreast for each two flights. This is an easy formation to fly when flying a straight course, and offers excellent cross cover.

When escorting several large boxes of bombers it is impossible to keep the group together, so squadrons and sections of squadrons are assigned a particular section of the task force. We usually fly two flights of four aeroplanes each together. The flights fly line abreast to offer cross cover, but if the lead ship is turning a lot it is necessary to fall in string. Normally, the flight leaders and element leaders look for bounces with the wingmen on the defensive. This doesn't mean that leaders never look back or wingmen never look down. It is impossible to see everything, but each pilot must keep his head moving and look to find.

When a member of the flight sees something suspicious, he calls it in and the leader takes the section to investigate. When it is identified as enemy, we notice the number and formation and try to make a surprise. The first flight of four goes down and the second flight stays up for top cover. It is necessary to have this protection, as a decent bounce cannot be made when trying to protect your own tail. If only one flight is in the vicinity, the second element acts as top cover. If a surprise can be made on several enemy aircraft, all ships in the flight can pick one out and drive up behind them and shoot them down. If

**Bare metal Mustangs of the 487th FS receive bombs at Bodney in the wake of the D-Day invasion. Note how the stripes had been left on the bottom of the wings but removed from the fuselage of both B-models visible in this photo. The aircraft parked behind the bomb truck is P-51B-15 42-106836, which was flown predominantly by Lt John Kessler. Like many other VIII Fighter Command groups temporarily assigned to supporting the invasion of western Europe, the 352nd FG suffered heavy losses at the hands of German mobile flak units whilst flying ground support missions inland from Normandy (*via Michael O'Leary*)**

the Hun sees you coming from above he usually starts diving and turning.

It is necessary for the wingman to stay with his leader, as the leader cannot follow the Hun through evasive action and do a good job of shooting unless the wingman is there to guard against attack by another enemy aircraft. Should the attacking flight or element get bounced, the wingman turns into the attack immediately and calls the leader.

When the leader is preparing to make a bounce, he should inform his squadron of his intentions. If a wingman sees an enemy aeroplane which would get away if he doesn't act immediately, he goes down on the bounce calling in as he does so. In this case the leader becomes the wingman.

When being bounced the first thing is always turn into the attack. The flight does not follow the leader into the turn, but each ship turns into the attackers.

If a pilot sees an enemy aircraft behind him in firing range he must take evasive action immediately. He slips and skids the ship as much as possible, giving the Hun maximum deflection. It is a good idea to turn in the direction of friendly aeroplanes so they can shoot or scare Jerry off your tail.

There will be times after a combat that you are down on the deck. If you are alone and can't find a friend to join with, the best thing to do is head for home, taking advantage of clouds for cover. If there are two

Capt John Francis 'Smiling Jack' Thornell poses with his crew chief, S/Sgt G A McIndoo, and their P-51B-15 42-106872 of the 328th FS/352nd FG in late June 1944. Thornell scored 17.25 aerial victories between 30 January and 21 June 1944, claiming no fewer than 11 of these kills in this very Mustang. He also claimed two aircraft damaged and two destroyed in strafing attacks. Note the fighter's highly-prized Spitfire rear-view mirror that helped compensate for the B-model's lack of rearward visibility (*via Michael O'Leary*)

Lt Robert H 'Punchy' Powell was forced to crash-land this aircraft (P-51B-15 42-106944) when its engine burst into flames seconds after he had taken off from Bodney on 18 July 1944. Fully fuelled for an escort mission, the fighter was consumed by fire (*via Sam Sox*)

or more they should climb back up providing they still have speed and gas. They should push everything to the firewall and keep speed in the climb – the leader must do a lot of turning in order to keep the men behind him up. Each man must be on the lookout for a bounce and watch each others' tail. If there are only two or three of you, you should find friends and join them.

As a conclusion, in escorting bombers, it is a good idea to range out to the sides, front and rear, and hit enemy fighters before they can get to the bomber formation, but do not run off on a wild goose chase and leave the bombers unprotected.

In all groups the policy as to who makes bounces and under what circumstances is arranged well beforehand and is thoroughly understood by all, in order to avoid indecision.

## George Earl 'Ratsy' Preddy Jr

George Preddy, who would become the top-scoring Mustang ace of World War 2, was born on 5 February 1919 in Greensboro, North Carolina. He obtained a civilian pilot's license during 1939 and barnstormed for a year before attempting to join the Navy as a pilot. After being rejected three times, he joined the Air Corps in 1940 and received his wings on 12 December 1941.

Preddy was assigned to the 49th FG and sent by ship to the South-west Pacific on 12 January 1942. Flying the Curtiss P-40E in combat for seven months, he was involved in a mid-air collision on 12 July 1942. Bailing out, Preddy was injured and spent three months in hospital before being transferred back to the USA after being released for training in the P-47.

On 28 December 1942 he was assigned to the 352nd FG and soon shipped out with the group to Britain. Becoming a captain with the 487th FS, Preddy scored three victories in December 1943/January 1944 with the P-47 prior to the unit transitioning onto the Mustang.

Once he had mastered the P-51, Preddy rapidly built his score, claiming 19 and three shared kills in just five months – including six Bf 109s on 6 August 1944. The ace was sent back to the USA soon after this spectacular haul, but returned to combat with the 352nd FG in October, taking command of the 328th FS on 28 October. On Christmas Day 1944, Preddy destroyed two Bf 109s near Koblenz and then attacked a low-flying Fw 190, but was in turn shot down and killed by American anti-aircraft fire. His final tally was 26.833 confirmed, three probables and four damaged.

This photograph of a very serious-looking Maj George Preddy was taken soon after he had arrived back in America on leave in August 1944. As with all leading aces returning home, his first stop was Washington, DC, where he spent 48 hours conducting interviews with the national Press. The officials of the various news bureaus who spoke with Preddy said that he 'made the best subject of any of the aces to come through Washington'. He had given them what they wanted, without having to embellish the truth (*via Roger Freeman*)

## Lt Col Everett W Stewart
## Executive Officer (Flying)
## 355th FG

In response to your letter I am submitting the following information drawn from my own experience, which I hope will be of some benefit to you.

### Individual Combat

In individual combat with P-51 aircraft against fighters, it is essential to move in quickly to firing range within the rapid acceleration of the P-51. If an enemy aircraft gets into a good dive before one can get into range, difficulty is usually encountered in closing. The P-51 and Me 109 seem to be about on par for dive and low altitude speed. The P-51 will out-turn the Me 109 at any altitude up to 25,000 ft (performance above that altitude is unknown). Greater difficulty is encountered in out-turning the Fw 190.

I believe that steep, uncoordinated turning is the best evasive action for the P-51 if the enemy aircraft is within firing range. When the turn is then tightened, an average pilot should be able to come into deflection shooting range of enemy aircraft by using a smooth, steep turn. Then, if the enemy aircraft elects to dive away the P-51 should be able to get astern of him. Luckily, I haven't had to use any violent evasive action as yet. If I try something that works, I'll let you know – if not, I'll probably be listed in the mission summary reports.

### Two-Ship Element

In attacking with two ships I like for my wingman to drop back to a position about 250 to 300 yards out to either side, and about 250 to 300 yards to the rear in such a position where he can completely cover the two of us from attack. I do not like for the wingman to be trying to shoot one down while I am shooting unless, of course, we are in some so-called "perfect" set-up. I prefer to give him the next victory and let me cover. My wingmen nearly always get to fire if I fire, and they usually come home with a victory.

This P-51B-5 (43-6999) of the Leiston-based 363rd FS/357th FG displays battle damage to its right wing in February 1944. Amongst the first Mustangs issued to the 357th FG upon the group's arrival in the ETO, this fighter was duly repaired and returned to service. It remained in the frontline until 17 August 1944, when it crashed at Middleton, just north of Leiston, killing its pilot, Lt Charles Campbell. This was the group's first pilot fatality due to a crash on British soil since it had commenced flying in the UK in November of 1943. Middleton Police Constable William Martin reported;
'Whilst the machine was in mid-air, the nearside wing became detached, the plane crashed and burst into flames immediately it struck the ground. The pilot was killed and the plane was totally destroyed. The wing fell a few hundred yards away. The machine fell in a field of wheat which was cut and shocked and owned by Walter Hatcher, Rose Farm, Middleton. About 40 shocks were destroyed by fire' (via Michael O'Leary)

125

Defensively, I like to have him fly as nearly line abreast as he can maintain. If the enemy aircraft actually attack, we break sharply into the attack and up, if possible. If we can thus get the advantage we can become offensive. If not, we just have to fight. If it is possible to get up into sun, the Hun will usually lose you, or keep going down.

### Four-Ship Flight

The four-ship flight is held together just as long as possible, both offensively and defensively.

The Hun definitely respects four-ships which will work together, and usually will not attack until he sees he has every other advantage, plus numbers of two or three to one. In attacking with four-ships the flight leader and the element leader move in to fire with the wingmen covering. Wingmen should stay with the leader until both have to split into a life and death dogfight. In flights deep into Germany, wingmen usually get their fighting and firing.

## General Information

1. From enemy coast to rendezvous, I like to keep the squadrons fairly compact in a close line abreast battle formation. This adds to better manoeuvring between and around flak areas, and prevents straggling flights and individuals. It is easier to fly than wide spread formations, and still affords pilots ample opportunity to look around.

2. Upon rendezvousing with bombers, I usually take the lead squadron over the lead portion of the bombers, with one section of eight on each side. Another squadron is despatched to the rear bomber units in the same manner, and both perform close escort. The top cover squadron is placed 2000 to 4000 ft above the bombers to watch the approach of enemy aircraft from above and far out. If an extremely large force is to be covered by one group, the third squadron is then placed on the centre section of the bombers fairly close.

3. In recent escort missions, flights and sections have quite frequently had to work independently along bombers, and use their own judgement on when to attack. They give a call if they have to

P-51B-10 43-7184 of the 362nd FS/357th FG features several modifications to the standard production aircraft. Firstly, it has a Spitfire rear-view mirror, secondly, a 'Malcolm hood', and thirdly a dorsal fin – the latter modification was rarely seen on B-model Mustangs (*via Michael O'Leary*)

Col Henry 'Russ' Spicer was the man chosen to lead the 357th FG into action in the ETO, joining the group on 17 February 1944, and claiming its first kill just three days later. On 22 February he downed two more fighters, but on 5 March he was forced to ditch in the Channel after his Mustang was struck by flak. Spicer was retrieved by the Germans and made a PoW. A career officer, Spicer had been flying with the army since 1934! (*via M O'Leary*)

The 364th FS's Lt Charles Sumner points to the nose-art on his P-51C-5 42-103502, much to the amusement of his groundcrew. This posed shot was taken at Leiston in the late spring of 1944. Sumner came agonisingly close to 'making ace', scoring 4.5 aerial kills and one damaged during his tour in the ETO (*via Michael O'Leary*)

leave for a bounce, or are bounced, and someone else is sent or moves into their area if possible.

4. Squadron and flight leaders will usually make the bounces until they get at least one victory, then we like to pass it around. If any leader fails to see a 'called in' aircraft, however, he will immediately despatch the individual who spots it after the enemy aircraft and give him cover.

5. If two flights can remain together on escort they will usually fly 500 to 1000 yards apart.

6. Flights use line abreast, with about 300 yards between individuals.

7. We find it quite difficult to get the squadrons back together after combat in recent encounters, as the Germans usually hit in large numbers, and there is plenty of combat and chasing to keep everyone busy.

8. On deep penetrations there is no need to scatter flights all over the sky. The Germans hit in large numbers at one portion of the bombers if they come up at all, and the more flights that can be kept close in to the bombers for call, the more people we can actually get into the initial fight.

### DEFENSIVE

1. When enemy aircraft are in a position to attack and we are free to fight, we try to climb to enemy aircraft and engage. As long as we can see the enemy aircraft, we do not feel that we are at a disadvantage.

2. From recent experience the size of the enemy's aircraft formation has not much influenced our response, except when it numbers less than 20, then we might send only one squadron in to attack or break up the attack. The more enemy aircraft in the formation the more we can shoot down.

3. On penetration and before rendezvous, enemy aircraft may start in attacking before tanks are dropped. If possible a small force will be despatched to break up enemy aircraft so others may continue to rendezvous. After rendezvous we usually drop tanks when enemy aircraft get in the immediate vicinity. Tanks are always kept as long as possible.

4. Radio transmission is used to designate assembly point for the group after a combat. We usually try to assemble over a certain part of the bombers.

5. We usually stay and fight with enemy aircraft, and hit the deck only when chasing enemy aircraft. If possible, it is always best to come out of enemy territory at above 15,000 ft.

**OFFENSIVE**
1. If I am in a favourable position I will usually take the first bounce myself. After that I will despatch any flight or element out that spots enemy aircraft. A rule of thumb cannot be set down for bouncing, as conditions right at that instant will govern just how you proceed with your attack.

2. I like to send about the same number down as there are enemy aircraft, with a flight or more as cover.

3. Our tactics when an enemy aircraft has the advantage is to usually head right for him and start a fight. We are usually able to stay together longer for teamwork than the Hun, and he will soon lose his advantage.

4. We try to keep one squadron with the bombers – and thus enable squadrons chasing enemy aircraft to stay with them until they are destroyed or widely dispersed – when they strike in forces of about 50 or more. Usually they will not strike with less than 50, and we seldom, if ever, find more than one such formation.

5. Every effort is made to engage enemy aircraft before they can get to the bombers. If they can be caught then, it is easier to get more of them as they are concentrating on the bombers and become more confused when attacked.

6. By making our presence immediately known to the Hun we can sometimes avert their attack entirely. And if he does indeed attack, it will usually be a feeble attack, giving us plenty of opportunity to pursue him.

'Ev' Stewart was one of only a handful of pilots to serve command postings with three fighter groups in the ETO. CO of the 352nd FG's 328th FS upon the group's arrival in England, he was posted to the 355th FG as its Executive Officer in January 1944. Made CO of the Steeple Morden-based group ten months later, Stewart was subsequently sent to lead the 4th FG in February 1945. Prior to his time in the ETO, he had already completed a tour of duty in the Pacific – which included being at Pearl Harbor on 7 December 1941! All of this frontline flying meant that 'Ev' Stewart participated in no less than 180 combat missions, totalling, 510 hours of 'stick time', during World War 2 (*via Michael O'Leary*)

7. While our formation is together the flight and element leaders may start a bounce, provided they call it in. If the leader does not desire them to continue the bounce or leave formation, they are immediately recalled. When we are with the bombers their liberty is extended.

## Everett W 'Stew' Stewart

Born on 18 July 1915 near Abilene, Kansas, Stewart went on to attend Kansas State University and then joined the Army Reserves as a flying cadet, being commissioned on 25 May 1939. In June of that year he was posted to the 79th PS/20th PG, and flew with the unit until early 1941. Promoted to first lieutenant on 10 October 1941, he was serving with the 20th PG in Hawaii on 7 December 1941 when the Japanese attacked – Stewart was later transferred to Midway Island.

By 10 October 1942 he was a major flying with the 328th FS/352nd FG in Britain, and in April 1943 he was made commanding officer of the squadron. Operating out of Bodney with P-47Ds, Stewart shared in the destruction of a Bf 110 on 22 December 1943, followed by a shared claim of He 177 two weeks later. On 23 January 1944 he was promoted to lieutenant colonel and subsequently transferred to the 355th FG as its deputy commander. Now flying P-51s, Stewart continued to add to his score, downing a Bf 109 on 6 March and a second confirmed Messerschmitt fighter destroyed (plus a damaged Bf 109 and a third as a probable) ten days later. After shooting down two trainers on 29 March, he became an ace.

On 4 November he became commander of the 355th and was made a full colonel on 18 January 1945. Stewart then moved to Debden on 21 February and assumed command of the 4th FG, damaging an Me 262 whilst leading the group on 3 March. After the war, he stayed in the air force and retired in January 1966. He died of a heart condition in San Antonio, Texas, on 10 February 1982.

'Stew' Stewart's final tally was 7.833 confirmed destroyed, one probable and four damaged, as well as 1.5 ground kills.

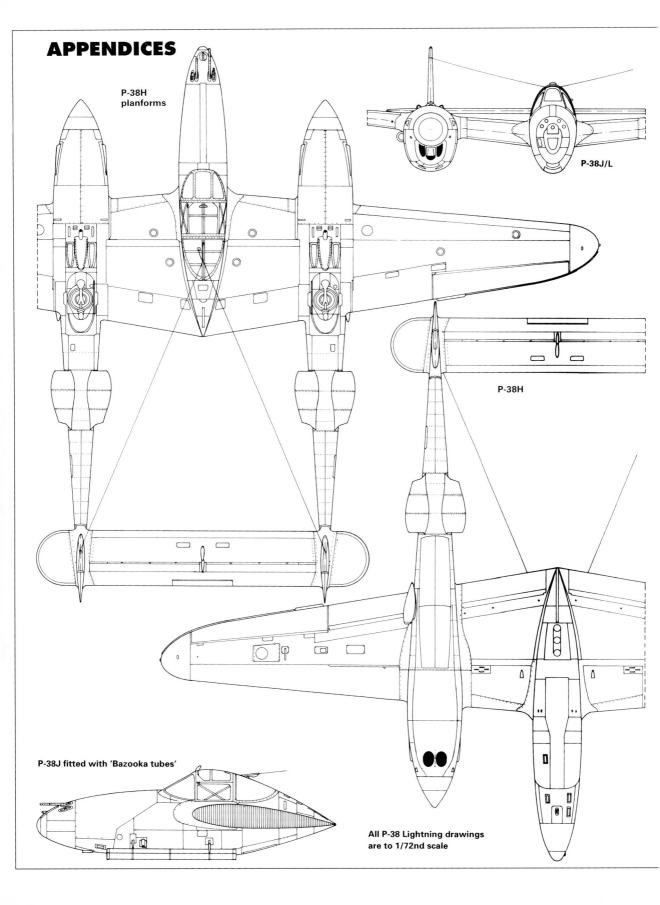

# APPENDICES

P-38H
planforms

P-38J/L

P-38H

P-38J fitted with 'Bazooka tubes'

All P-38 Lightning drawings
are to 1/72nd scale

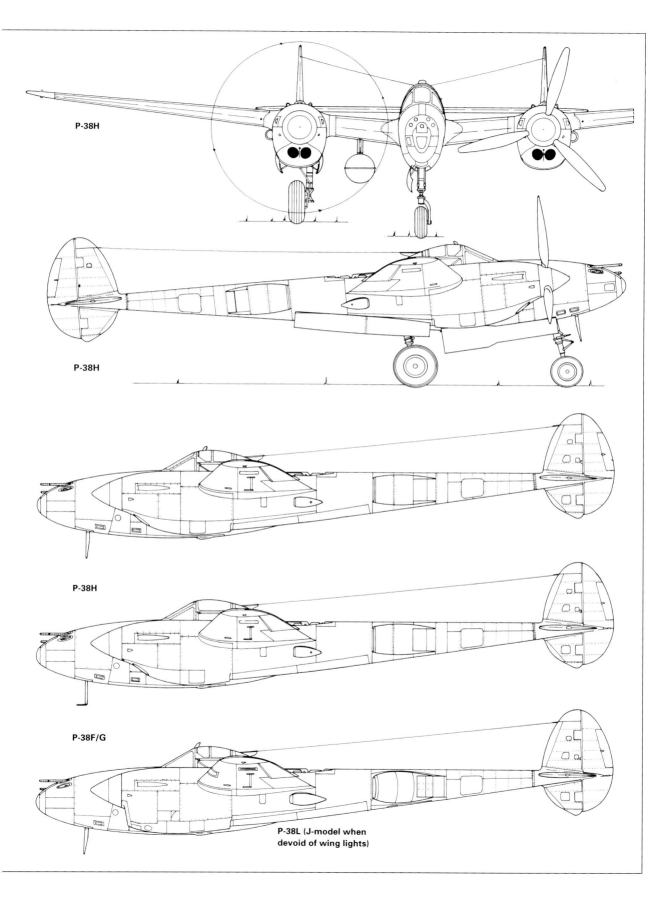

P-38H

P-38H

P-38H

P-38F/G

P-38L (J-model when
devoid of wing lights)

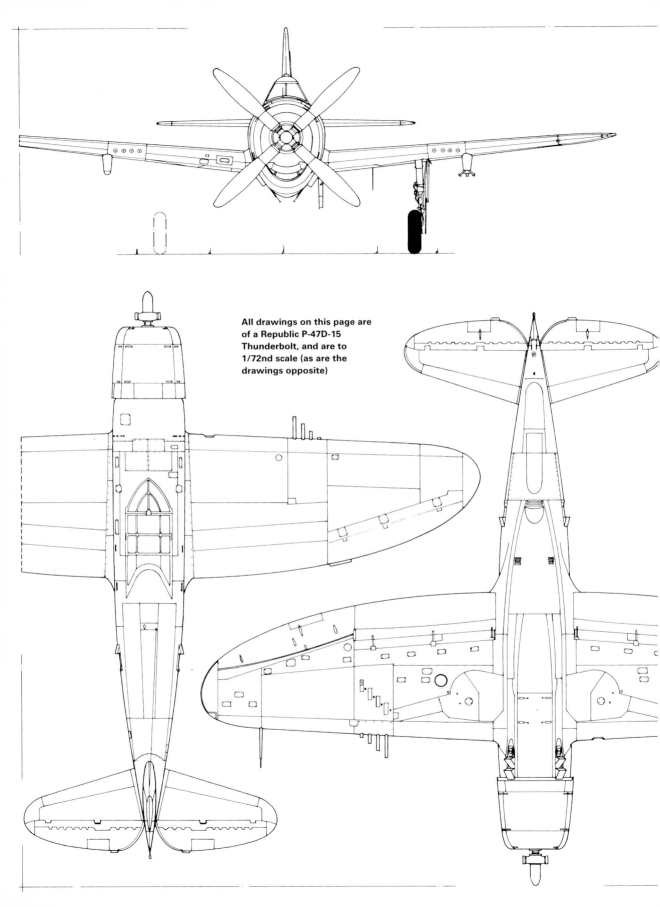

All drawings on this page are
of a Republic P-47D-15
Thunderbolt, and are to
1/72nd scale (as are the
drawings opposite)

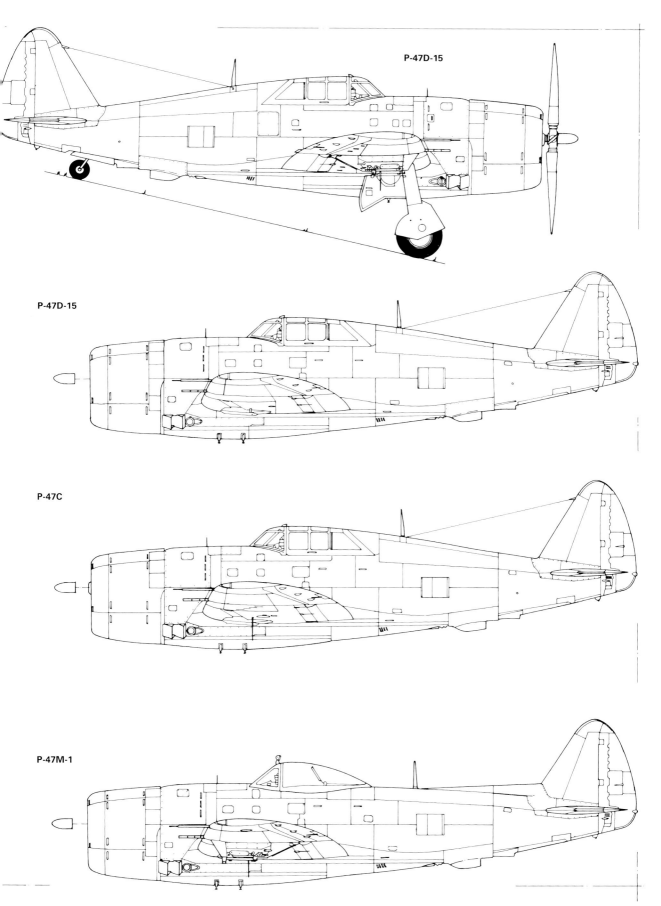

P-47D-15

P-47D-15

P-47C

P-47M-1

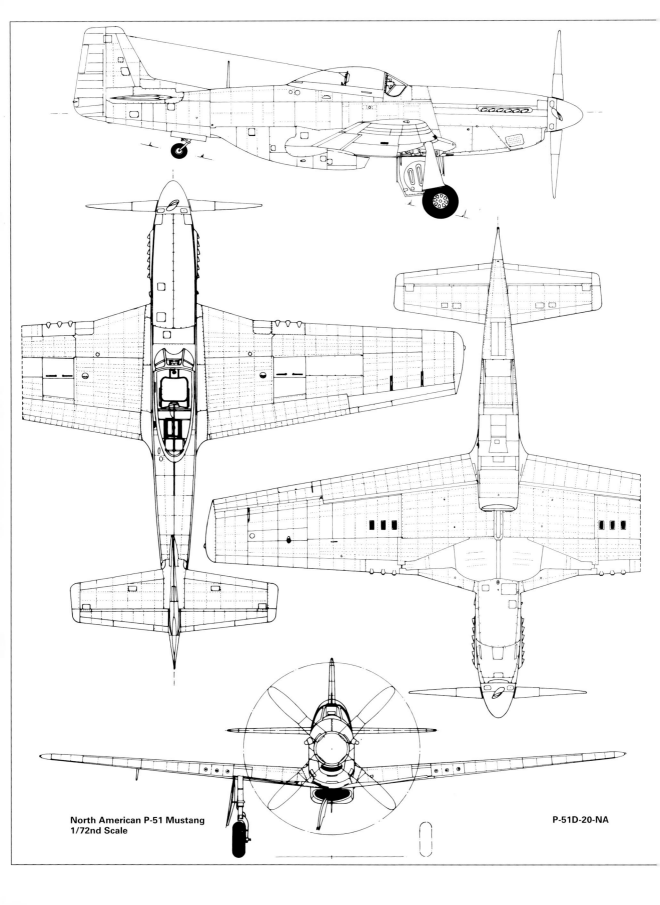

**North American P-51 Mustang**
**1/72nd Scale**

P-51D-20-NA

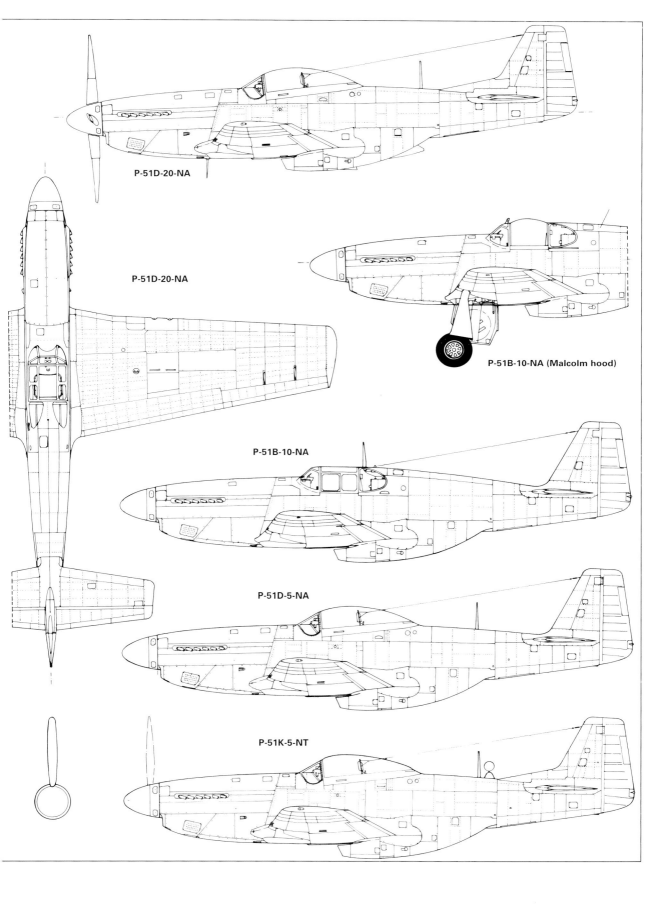

P-51D-20-NA

P-51D-20-NA

P-51B-10-NA (Malcolm hood)

P-51B-10-NA

P-51D-5-NA

P-51K-5-NT

# COLOUR PLATES

## 1

**P-47C-5 41-6335/*EL JEEPO* of Capt Charles London, 83rd FS/78th FG, Duxford, June 1943**

This famous aircraft was used by VIII FC's premier ace Capt Charles London to score all five of his kills, one probable and two damaged between 14 May and 30 July 1943 – a fifth swastika was added to the tally seen here following his 'ace making' double haul on the 30th. *EL JEEPO* experienced no paint changes in the few months that London flew it.

## 2

**P-47C-5 41-6330/*"MOY TAVARISH"* of Col Hubert Zemke, CO of the 56th FG, Horsham St Faith, June 1943**

The personal aircraft of Col Hub Zemke, and flown by him on most of his early missions, this Thunderbolt bore the legend *"MOY TAVARISH"* ("My Comrade") for a few weeks in the spring of 1943. This reflected Zemke's time in the USSR with an RAF party during 1941. The big fighter also carried the ID letter code 'Z', which denoted the surname of the pilot, and was a privilege of rank afforded to flight, squadron and group commanders only. The name, victory symbols and spoked wheel motif seen in this profile were removed during the summer of 1943, as the colonel felt uneasy about the CO displaying such individualism. On 21 September 1943 Zemke had this aircraft moved from the 62nd to the 63rd FS for maintenance in furtherance of his wish not to be seen as favouring one squadron. Three of Zemke's credited victories were obtained with this fighter, which was coded UN-S when in the 63rd. It was struck from the squadron's records after Lt Adam Wisniewski bellied the P-47 in at Manston on Christmas Eve 1943.

## 3

**P-47C-5 41-6630/*Spokane Chief* of Maj Eugene Roberts, CO of the 84th FS/78th FG, Duxford, August 1943**

Maj Roberts was able to use this aircraft to achieve six of his nine confirmed kills, plus the solitary probable that he kicked off his tally with on 1 July 1943. The ace's opening trio of kills were then scored in P-47C-2 41-6240/WZ-E, before returning to his *Spokane Chief* for – as far as is known – the aircraft's first confirmed victory on 17 August. CO of the 84th FS for much of his frontline tour, Eugene Roberts was subsequently promoted to lieutenant colonel in October 1943 and given the position of Deputy Group CO. By the time he was posted to a desk job in VIII Fighter Command HQ, he had flown 89 missions.

## 4

**P-47C-5 41-6584/*HOLY JOE* of Lt Joe Egan, 63rd FS/56th FG, Halesworth, August 1943**

Seen in standard P-47 camouflage and early ETO markings, this aircraft was used by five-victory ace Lt Joe Egan to down his first kill (an Fw 190) on 19 August 1943. This was the second C-model to be assigned to Egan, the first having been written off after a crash-landing in May 1943. All of his remaining victories were scored in P-47D-10 42-75069/UN-E and P-47D-15 42-75855/UN-E. *HOLY JOE* ended its service with the 56th when the fighter crash-landed on 1 December 1943.

## 5

**P-47C-2 41-6211/*JACKIE* of Capt Robert Lamb, 61st FS/56th FG, Halesworth, August 1943**

Like Joe Egan, future seven-kill ace Capt Robert Lamb used this aircraft to claim his first victory on 19 August (again an Fw 190). He was still flying it in mid-October, when he claimed an 'Me 210' damaged on the 18th. *JACKIE* failed to return from a bomber escort mission to Solingen on 1 December 1943 whilst being flown by Lt Jack Brown.

## 6

**P-47C-5 41-6343/*LITTLE COOKIE* of Capt Walter Cook, 62nd FS/56th FG, Halesworth, October 1943**

Capt Walter Cook scored four of his six victories in this P-47C-5, which was his assigned aircraft – it bore the name *LITTLE COOKIE* on both sides of the cowling. His remaining two kills (a pair of Fw 190s) were achieved on 11 November 1943 in P-47C-2 41-6193/LM-B, which he had been forced to use after *LITTLE COOKIE* suffered a flat tyre and subsequent propeller damage when landing on 20 October 1943. After repairs 41-6343 was retired to a training unit. Cook completed 66 missions before returning to the USA in February 1944.

## 7

**P-47C-2 41-6259 of Lt Glen Schiltz, 63rd FS/56th FG, Halesworth, October 1943**

This aircraft was assigned to Glen Schiltz from 8 February 1943 to 18 January 1944, when it was retired to Northern Ireland. The fighter later became a hack aircraft of the 65th Fighter Wing, being based at Debden. Schiltz obtained five of his eight credited victories with this P-47, including his opening trio of kills (all Fw 190s) on 17 August 1943. On 11 January 1944 he was credited with a second triple-victory haul, although this time he was flying 41-6259's replace-ment, P-47D-11 42-75232/UN-Z.

## 8

**P-47D-1 42-7877/*"JACKSON COUNTY, MICHIGAN., FIGHTER"/IN THE MOOD* of Capt Gerald Johnson, 61st FS/56th FG, Halesworth, October 1943**

A captain by the time he used this particular Thunderbolt to score 5.5 aerial victories, Gerald W Johnson was one of the 'Wolfpack's' most outstanding pilots. Assigned to Gerry Johnson, he used this War Bond P-47 to claim his first confirmed victory on 26 June 1943 (an Fw 190), and he continued to fly the fighter until the end of 1943, although his final kill with the aircraft was scored on 14 October (another Fw 190). All Johnson's P-47s were 'razorbacks', and he achieved kills in at least five different aircraft.

## 9

**P-47D-1 42-7938/*"HEWLETT-WOODMERE LONG ISLAND"* of Maj David Schilling, Deputy CO of the 56th FG, Halesworth, October 1943**

Schilling's second assigned combat aircraft carried the dedication *"HEWLETT-WOODMERE LONG ISLAND"*, who were purchasers of War Bonds to the value of a P-47, on the left side of the fuselage. One of four pilots in the group to score in excess of 20 aerial kills, Schilling claimed three and one shared in this Thunderbolt, the first (an Fw 190) on 8 October 1943. In January 1944 Schilling took over a new

D-11, and 42-7938 was passed to another pilot and the 'plane-in-squadron' letter changed from <u>S</u> to S. The aircraft ended its days with the 56th on 3 February 1944 when its pilot carried out a forced landing in a field after exhausting his fuel towards the end of a mission.

## 10

**P-47C-5 41-6325/ 'Lucky Little Devil' of Lt John Vogt, 63rd FS/56th FG, Halesworth, October 1943**

John Vogt was one of a number of VIII Fighter Command pilots who downed enemy aircraft while flying the same type of fighter with more than one group – in his case the 56th and 356th FGs. This P-47C-5 was his first assigned aircraft in the 56th, and he used it to score his first three victories. Vogt also flew a P-47D-20 and finally a D-25 'bubbletop' after transferring to the 360th FS/356th FG in late February 1944, the ace claiming his last three kills with this group for a final tally of 8-0-1. 41-6325 also transferred out of the 56th FG during the winter of 1944, leaving Halesworth in late January.

## 11

**P-47C-2 41-6271/ Rat Racer of Lt Frank McCauley, 61st FS/56th FG, Halesworth, October 1943**

One of the 56th FG's early aces, 'Mac' McCauley was allocated this P-47C-2, which he named *Rat Racer* (the words appear under the portrait of Mighty Mouse, just above the wing root), in the summer of 1943. He scored all of his 5.5 aerial kills in this aircraft, the P-47 exhibiting six victory symbols (one was later disallowed). After completing 46 missions, McCauley left the 'Wolfpack' on 20 November 1943 and served out the war as an instructor with the 495th Fighter Training Group.

## 12

**P-47D-6 42-74641/ Feather Merchant II of Maj Jack Price, CO of the 84th FS/78th FG, Duxford, November 1943**

Capt Jack Price was assigned this P-47 in the spring of 1943, and he was able to gain the last two of his five victories whilst flying it. He had earlier used three different Thunderbolts (C-2s 41-6270/WZ-A and 41-6228/WZ-N, and C-5 41-6333/WZ-V) to score his first three kills. At some stage in the autumn of 1943 reports suggest that the individual code letter of this aircraft changed from 'Z' to 'A', although this remains unconfirmed.

## 13

**P-47C-5 41-6347/ TORCHY/ "LIL" AbNER" of Capt Eugene O'Neill, 62nd FS/56th FG, Halesworth, November 1943**

Capt Gene O'Neill used this P-47C-5 to score his first 3.5 victories in November/December 1943 – the fraction was a Bf 110 he jointly shot down on 26 November 1943. The aircraft also carried a third name – *Jessie O* – on the starboard side adjacent to the cockpit. Having joined the 62nd PS on 23 December 1941 (it was then still designated a pursuit squadron), O'Neill used P-47D-10 42-75125/ LM-<u>E</u> to claim his final kill on 6 February 1944. Although he is listed as an ace in numerous publications, O'Neill is credited by both the USAF Historical Study 85 and VIII Fighter Command Final Assessment credit with 4.5 kills, both organisations having failed to find any record of that elusive fifth victory that would have made him an ace.

## 14

**P-38H-5 42-67027 of Lt Gerald A Brown, 38th FS/55th FG, Nuthampstead, November 1943**

On 13 November 1943 Jerry Brown (flying this aircraft) and Capt Joe Myers comprised one of the elements put up by the 55th FG to escort bombers on a particularly rough mission to Bremen. Brown had already succeeded in damaging an attacking Bf 109 short of the bomber stream when another fighter latched onto his tail and pumped cannon and machine-gun fire into the hapless P-38. Seeing his squadronmate's predicament, Myers managed to shoot the determined German off his colleague's tail, allowing Brown to somehow coax his gravely damaged P-38 home. Once back at Nuthampstead, the bullet-riddled Lightning was the source of much amazement for Lockheed and USAAF technical experts alike, who counted in excess of 100 holes in the aircraft's fuselage caused by bullet and cannon strikes. Going on to fly P-38J-10s, Jerry Brown subsequently destroyed a Bf 109 at high altitude on 31 January 1944, an Fw 190 on 18 March, another Bf 109 on 8 April and a He 111 and a second Fw 190 exactly a week later.

## 15

**P-38H-5 42-67064/ Texas Ranger of Col Jack Jenkins, Deputy CO 55th FG, Nuthampstead, November 1943**

The first victories to fall to the P-38 in north-west Europe were scored by the 55th FG on 3 November 1943, future group commander Jack Jenkins claiming a Bf 109 shot down and an Fw 190 probably destroyed. It would seem from a post-war examination of JG 1's records that Jenkins could actually have claimed both fighters destroyed, as the *jagdgeschwader* admitted the loss of two fighters in action with P-38s on this day. The colonel tasted success in *Texas Ranger* just once more, using the Lightning to destroy an Fw 190 22 days after his 'double' haul. Jenkins led the first American fighters over Berlin on 3 March 1944 when the 55th FG ranged over the German capital – his P-38 on this occasion was *Texas Ranger IV*. This artwork was carried by at least two of Jenkins' P-38s, having been painted by talented artist Sgt Bob Sand, who worked in the propeller shop at Nuthampstead. He decorated five 55th FG Lightnings during his time with the group, and in respect to this particular 'commission' Sands stated years after the war, 'My main memory is of working on this all night a couple of nights running, and of my boss's displeasure at my not showing up for work until 9 am'.

## 16

**P-47D-5 42-8634/ Dove of Peace IV of Lt Col Glenn Duncan, CO of the 353rd FG, Metfield, December 1943**

Glenn Duncan had an outstanding career with the 353rd FG, and he flew at least four P-47s to score a total of 19.5 victories. The D-5 depicted here was apparently named *Dove of Peace IV*, although the exact location of the name (on the starboard side) has been impossible to trace. The fact that this aircraft was number four means that there were three others during Duncan's long career, although they were not all necessarily P-47s. He had served briefly with the 361st FG before transferring to the 353rd on 14 March 1943, which suggests that the other *'Doves'* may have been aircraft flown in the USA prior to his move overseas.

## 17

**P-47D-1 42-7883/*IRON ASS* of Maj Jack Oberhansly, CO of the 82nd FS/78th FG, Duxford, December 1943**

The second P-47 assigned to Jack Oberhansly, this aircraft bears the modified form of his personal insignia. Previously, Oberhansly had flown C-5 41-6542/MX-W, which carried the same name on the port side, but in a square. The aircraft depicted was used by Oberhansly to score two kills and a probable on 27 September and 30 November 1943, the pilot then using P-47D-11 42-75406/MX-Z to achieve his next four successes. Oberhansly's sixth, and last, kill came in 'bubbletop' D-28 44-19566/MX-X on 28 August 1944.

## 18

**P-47D-11 42-75435/*Hollywood High Hatter* of Lt Paul Conger, 61st FS/56th, Halesworth, December 1943**

This grandly-named Thunderbolt was used by Paul Conger as a replacement for his originally assigned War Bond subscription P-47D-1 42-7880/HV-N *"REDONDO BEACH, CALIFORNIA"*. The ace was almost certainly responsible for the three kill marks displayed under the cockpit of this fighter, which was subsequently transferred to the Boxted-based Air Sea Rescue Squadron in May 1944. Conger completed two tours with the 56th FG, finishing up flying P-47M-1 44-21134/UN-P. Like many other aces, he used at least three P-47s not assigned to him to reach his final tally of 11.5 kills.

## 19

**P-47D-10 42-75163 of Lt Joe Powers, 61st FS/56th FG, Halesworth, December 1943**

Joe Powers received this aircraft as a replacement for C-2 41-6267/HV-V in early December 1943, having claimed single kills both in the former P-47 and C-5 41-6337/HV-S (both Bf 109s). His first victories in the D-10, which he named *Powers Girl*, came on 11 December when he destroyed a Bf 109 and a Bf 110, and damaged a second *Zerstörer*. Powers subsequently flew a number of missions mostly in other P-47s (including 41-6267 yet again), although he did score kills in *Powers Girl* in January, February and March 1944. A captain by the time his tour ended in May 1944, Joe Powers' final tally was 14.5-0-5.

## 20

**P-47D-5 42-8476/*LITTLE DEMON* of Capt Walter Beckham, 351st FS/353rd FG, Metfield, December 1943**

Walt Beckham had *LITTLE DEMON* assigned to him at the beginning of his ETO tour, and it is assumed that he scored the majority of his total of 18 victories in it. He is not known to have been assigned any other Thunderbolt while serving with the 353rd FG, although when he was shot down by flak on 22 February 1944, he was flying D-11 42-75226.

## 21

**P-47D-11 42-75510 of Lt Col Francis Gabreski, CO of the 61st FS/56th FG, Halesworth, January 1944**

'Gabby' Gabreski's P-47D-11 42-75510 was a remarkably plain fighter, being adorned with standard VIII Fighter Command white recognition bands. The ace's score stood at eight victories at this point in his tour, 42-75510 being the third Republic fighter to be assigned to Gabreski following his arrival in the ETO in early 1943.

## 22

**P-47D-1 42-7890 *BOISE BEE* of Lt Duane Beeson, 334th FS/4th FG, Debden, January 1944**

This aircraft was responsible for the destruction of no fewer than 11 enemy fighters whilst flown by Duane 'Bee' Beeson, who finished the war as one of the highest scoring VIII Fighter Command pilots with 17.333 kills by April 1944. He transitioned onto the P-51 in late February 1944, taking a tally of 12 kills scored on P-47s with him – Beeson was easily the ranking Thunderbolt ace within the 4th FG.

## 23

**P-47D-11 42-75242 of Capt Michael Quirk, 62nd FS/56th FG, Halesworth, February 1944**

Mike Quirk had used P-47C-2 41-6215/LM-K and D-2 42-22481/LM-J to score his first three kills prior to being assigned this P-47D-11. He went on to claim 6.5-1-1 in this aircraft, the last of which was downed on 25 February 1944 (an Fw 190). The Thunderbolt's overpainted tail band indicates a transition to coloured tactical markings, which this aircraft duly received while Quirk was still its regular pilot. He rose in rank to major on 17 September 1944 , but by that time he had already been a PoW for a week after being downed by flak over Seligenstadt airfield on the 10th of the month. Quirk's final tally was 11-1-1.

## 24

**P-47D-5 42-8413/*"MA" FRAN 3rd* of Capt Norman Olson, 357th FS/355th FG, Steeple Morden, February 1944**

Capt Norman Olson scored 6-0-2 during the 355th FG's brief seven-month association with the Republic fighter in the ETO. Although not definitely confirmed, it is presumed that this particular D-5 was the only P-47 assigned to the ace, although he also used a D-2 and a D-6 to achieve his full score. Having transitioned to the P-51B in late March, Olson was killed on 8 April 1944 when his Mustang was shot down by flak near Celle Hofer.

## 25

**P-47D-5 42-8461/*"Lucky"* of Lt Robert Johnson, 61st FS/56th FG, Halesworth, February 1944**

Robert S Johnson's third assigned aircraft, *"Lucky"* was used to score his third, fourth, fifth and sixth victories before being lost in the North Sea on 22 March 1944 with Dale Stream at the controls. Johnson had previously flown two C-model Thunderbolts, christened *Half Pint* and *All Hell*, and had shot down his first two kills in the latter aircraft, C-5 41-6235/HV-P. Following the loss of 42-8461, Johnson was assigned D-15 42-76234/HV-P.

## 26

**P-38J-10 42-67717/*My Dad* of Capt James M Morris, 77th FS/20th FG, King's Cliffe, February 1944**

Although P-38J-10 42-67717 was the aircraft adorned with 'Slick' Morris's impressive tally, he only claimed one of his 7.333 victories with it – a Bf 110 downed over Schweinfurt on 24 February 1944. He was the Eighth Air Force's first P-38 ace, and he scored 5.333 of his kills in J-10 42-67871. Four of these came in a single sortie on 8 February 1944, the two Fw 190s and two Bf 109Gs he downed on this mission setting a scoring record at the time for the P-38 in the ETO.

Morris scored his final kill (an Me 410) in P-38J-15 43-28397 on 7 July 1944, but the Lightning was in turn so badly shot up by the stricken fighter's remote-controlled waist guns that he too was forced to bail out – he spent the rest of the war as a PoW.

## 27

### P-47D-5 42-8487/ "SPIRIT OF ATLANTIC CITY, N.J." of Capt Walker Mahurin, 63rd FS/56th FG, Halesworth, March 1944

Capt 'Bud' Mahurin shot down a total of 19.75 aircraft, ranging from Fw 190s to a Ju 88, during his lengthy career with the 56th FG. This War Bond presentation aircraft (the second assigned to Mahurin) was used for all but three of these victories – the first two (Fw 190s) were achieved in C-2 41-6259/UN-V on 17 August, and he claimed a Bf 109 (and a second damaged) in D-11 42-75278/UN-B on 29 November. Unusual in that it retained its full squadron code letters (the inscription tended to replace the two letters on other subscriber-purchased P-47s), this machine is not known to have had any other form of personal marking on the starboard side. Mahurin was eventually shot down in it on 27 March 1944 by the rear gunner of a Do 217 that he had helped destroy south of Chartres.

## 28

### P-47D-5 42-8473 Sweet LOUISE/ Mrs Josephine/ Hedy of Capt Virgil Meroney, 487th FS/352nd FG, Bodney, March 1944

Virgil Meroney was the first, and only, pilot to 'make ace' while the Bodney group flew the P-47, his score being an impressive nine kills and one damaged over a period of some three-and-a-half months between 1 December 1943 and 16 March 1944 – all of these victories were scored in this P-47. The above quoted names were, in order, Meroney's wife, Crew Chief S/Sgt Giesting's wife and Sgt Gillenwater's wife. The last name appeared on the starboard cowling, while Mrs Josephine was painted on a slant in approximately the same place as Sweet Louise. Yet another ace downed by flak, Meroney was lost whilst flying one of his first sorties in a P-51B on 8 April 1944. He spent the rest of the war as a PoW.

## 29

### P-47D-6 42-74753/ OKIE of Lt Quince Brown, 84th FS/78th FG, Duxford, March 1944

Quince Brown's final tally of 12.333 kills was obtained in just under a year of combat operations between 27 September 1943 and 1 September 1944. This aircraft is his originally-assigned Thunderbolt, which he used to score 7.333 of his kills, including his first six successes – Brown also destroyed enemy aircraft in three other Thunderbolts, namely D-6 42-74723/WZ-X, D-5 42-8574/WZ-D- and D-25 42-26567/WZ-V. OKIE (the nickname perpetuated Brown's Oklahoma background) reverted to another pilot with the ID code 'V' following Brown's receipt of natural-metal 'razorback' D-5 42-8574/WZ-D.

## 30

### P-47D-6 42-74750/ Lady Jane of Lt John Truluck, 63rd FS/56th FG, Halesworth, March 1944

John 'Lucky' Truluck scored his first kill in P-47D-1 42-7853/UN-R, before using the aircraft depicted here to claim his second and third victories. He then enjoyed success with D-5 42-8488/UN-A on 26 November (an Fw 190 destroyed and a Bf 110 damaged), before reverting back to Lady Jane to 'make ace' on 24 February 1944 with an Fw 190 kill. Truluck claimed his sixth kill in D-10 42-75206/UN-G, although he again went back to Lady Jane to score his seventh, and final, victory (an Fw 190), plus a damaged (a Bf 109), on 15 March 1944.

## 31

### P-47D-15 42-76179/ Little Chief of Lt Frank Klibbe, 61st FS/56th FG, Halesworth, March 1944

Lt Frank Klibbe decorated at least two of his P-47s with a Red Indian head motif, complete with war bonnet and the wording Little Chief. This was the third Thunderbolt assigned to him, and he is believed to have scored four of his seven kills in it. Klibbe's missions with the 56th FG's 61st FS totalled 63.

## 32

### P-47D-10 42-75207/ Rozzie Geth/ "BOCHE BUSTER" of Lt Fred Christensen, 62nd FS/56th FG, Halesworth, March 1944

Although this aircraft was the first P-47 assigned to Fred Christensen, the 62nd FS's future ranking ace actually claimed his first of 21.5 kills in C-2 41-6193/LM-B. However, his next 10.5 victories were all downed in this D-10, which he continued to use until the late June 1944. Christensen flew a further two 'razorbacks' during his 107-mission tour.

## 33

### P-47D-10 42-75214/ POLLY of Lt David Thwaites, 361st FS/ 356th FG, Martlesham Heath, March 1944

David Thwaites was the only pilot in the 356th FG to score all his kills on the P-47 while serving with this group. Naming both his assigned Thunderbolts (the second being P-47D-20 42-76457/QI-L) POLLY, Thwaites is known to have used at least three P-47s to achieve his haul of 6-0-3. Following the completion of his tour in September 1944, he returned to the USA and became an instructor.

## 34

### P-38J-10 42-67926/ Susie of Capt Lindol F Graham, 79th FS/20th FG, King's Cliffe, March 1944

The 79th FS was blessed with a number of skilled Lightning pilots, but Capt 'Lindy' Graham was considered to be the 'pick of the bunch'. Rookie pilots looked up to him as the example to follow, for he had been with the unit since its arrival in the frontline, and had scored 5.5 victories in under three months. Thus, when Graham was killed in Susie on 18 March 1944, the unit felt it as a body blow. Graham's 'big day' in combat was 29 January, when he downed three Fw 190s in two separate engagements on the same bomber escort mission whilst flying J-10 42-67497. He went on to 'make ace' in the fighter depicted in this profile during a confused aerial clash involving several P-38s and a formation of Bf 110s on 20 February south-west of Brunswick – he claimed two Messerschmitt 'twins' destroyed. The red star painted beneath the fighter's nickname (and the attendant white scroll to its immediate right) was worn in honour of a former Lockheed employee killed in action during World War 2 – these markings were to be found on a number of P-38s, having been carefully applied at the factory immediately prior to the aircraft being delivered to the USAAF. The white Eighth Air Force group recognition symbol on the tail was not added to the P-38 until early March 1944.

## 35

### P-51B-5 43-6913/*Shangri-La* of Capt Don Gentile, 336th FS/4th FG, Debden, March 1944

Winner of the 'Ace Race' to reach Eddie Rickenbacker's 26-kill mark from World War 1 (the 4th FG ace claimed 21.833 aerial and 6 ground kills), Gentile's personal success, and Gen Dwight Eisenhower's remark that the youngster from Ohio was a 'one-man air force', obscure his contribution as a team player. Indeed, his unselfish partnership with wingman John T Godfrey proved mutually beneficial, for the latter pilot achieved 16.333 aerial and 12.666 ground kills (admittedly, only half of these were claimed whilst Gentile was with the 4th FG). Initially rejected for pilot training by the Army Air Corps, Gentile followed the example of many of his compatriots and joined the RCAF. Posted to England, he scored his first two kills – and received a British DFC – as a member of No 133 'Eagle' Sqn flying Spitfires over the ill-fated Dieppe landing force on 19 August 1942. Gentile transferred to the AAF, along with the rest of his squadron, the following month, and by the time he had converted onto Mustangs in early March 1944, he had claimed two victories in Spitfires and 4.333 in the P-47. The ace enjoyed great success in the few brief weeks that he flew the P-51 in action claiming triple victory hauls on 3 and 8 March and 8 April – the latter two whilst flying this very aircraft. Meticulously marked by his groundcrew, and well photographed by the AAF's Press Corps, *Shangri-La* had its back broken when Gentile hit the Debden runway during a low-level pass (primarily flown for the attendant Press) to celebrate his final mission on 13 April 1944. It was just as well that Gentile had finished his tour, for the 4th FG's CO, the legendary Col Don Blakeslee, had stated that anyone who 'pranged a kite while stunting' would be immediately kicked out of the group. Once back home, Gentile was issued with a silver P-51D painted in similar markings, which he used as personal transport during a bond-drive tour of the USA.

## 36

### P-51B-5 Mustang 43-6819/*BEE* of Capt Duane W 'Bee' Beeson, CO of the 334th FS/4th FG, Debden, April 1944

One of the first P-51Bs issued to the 4th FG, this aircraft is finished in the standard overall olive drab (OD) over neutral grey undersurfaces which remained in favour until mid-1944. The colours were applied in such a way that they would gradually blend into one another through the use of slight overspray. White recognition stripes were also painted across the wings, tailplane, fin and around the nose, although these were removed during the course of March-April 1944. As with most other P-51Bs in the 4th FG, 43-6819 had its white nose marking oversprayed with red (the 4th FG's colour) in mid-March. The paint had been purchased locally, and the pigment content was so low that groundcrews had to apply up to six coats to fully obscure the white marking beneath it. The white fin and tail bands seen on the aircraft in Iain

Wyllie's specially-commissioned cover artwork for this volume were immediately painted out upon Beeson's return to Debden in the wake of the 23 March 1944 mission. All of 'Bee' Beeson's Mustang kills were claimed in this aircraft, and he was also flying it when shot down by flak on 5 April.

## 37

### P-47D-10 42-75068 of Lt Raymond Wetmore, 370th FS/359th FG, East Wretham, April 1944

Although Lt Ray Wetmore of the 359th FG fell just short of being a full P-47 ace with a total score of 4.25, his aircraft is included here to represent the group. The highest scoring Thunderbolt pilot in the 359th, his closest rival was Lt Robert Booth of the 369th FS, who was credited with four kills. Two of Wetmore's haul (Fw 190s) were scored on 16 March 1944 in this aircraft, and he used two other P-47s (D-5 42-8663/CR-G and C-2 41-6282/CS-O) to claim his remaining successes. The eight-kill tally marked on the fighter is something of a mystery, as even by including all of Wetmore's reported claims (six in P-47s) as confirmed kills, this still does not match up with the symbols shown. The explanation must surely be that another pilot enjoyed success while flying this P-47. Ray Wetmore went on to claim a further 17 kills with the Mustang following his group's transition to the North American fighter in early May 1944.

## 38

### P-47D-21 42-25512/*Penrod and Sam* of Capt Robert Johnson, 62nd FS/56th FG, Boxted, May 1944

Robert S Johnson's last P-47 was named for his groundcrew as a tribute to their outstanding work. He used up to four P-47s during his time in the ETO, one of which was lost whilst being flown by another pilot. This aircraft wore the Johnson's final score, which bettered that of World War 1 ace Eddie Rickenbacker by a single kill.

## 39

### P-38J-15 43-104308/*'Gentle Annie'* of Col Harold J Rau, CO of the 20th FG, King's Cliffe, April 1944

Although this machine wears Col Rau's full kill tally, it was not the P-38 he used on 8 April 1944 to lead a last-minute fighter sweep over Germany during which he scored all his victories, and his group won a Distinguished Unit Citation. Rau managed to down one Bf 109, as well as confirm four unidentified twin-engined aircraft destroyed on the ground during the course of this memorable mission. 20th FG aces Morris and Fiebelkorn also claimed ground victories on 8 April. 43-104308 was lost during a strafing mission when hit by flak over Le Treport on 16 June 1944, its pilot, Lt Earl O Smith, managing to evade capture.

## 40

### P-51B-5 43-6636/*ILL-WIND?* of 1Lt Nicholas 'Cowboy' Megura, 334th FS/4th FG, Debden, April 1944

Double ace Megura claimed at least three and two shared victories in this factory-camouflaged P-51B in March-April 1944. With his score standing at 11.833 aerial victories and 3.75 strafing kills, the 'Cowboy's' promising combat career came to a sudden halt on 22 May 1944 when his Mustang (43-7158) was shot up in error by an over-zealous P-38. With his glycol tank seriously holed, Megura was forced to crash-land in neutral Sweden, where he was interned until 28 June. Megura was prevented from returning to action in the ETO following his repatriation due to the rules of his previous internment, and was posted back to the USA. On most early camouflaged (and some natural metal) Mustangs the specified white nose recognition band gave way to group colours (red for the 4th FG for example) in early 1944, while the tailfin stripe was deleted altogether because it broke up the distinctive outline of the Mustang's tail. White stripes (black on natural metal aircraft) were retained on the wings and tailplane into early spring, however. This particular aircraft was lost 13 days prior to Megura's internment when shot down by flak on 9 May 1944 during a strafing attack on Reims/Champagne airfield, its pilot, 1Lt Vernon 'Cub' Burroughs, being made a PoW.

## 41

### P-51B-10 43-7172/*Thunder Bird* of 1Lt Ted Lines, 335th FS/4th FG, Debden, April 1944

Lines, from Mesa, Arizona, decorated his Mustangs with appropriate American Indian-style artwork, and bestowed the name *Thunder Bird* on each of them. With ten officially credited aerial victories and another three awarded by the 4th FG, but not recognised by the Victory Credits Board (none were scored in this particular Mustang, however), Lines was a little-publicised member of the Debden-based group. Replaced by one of the first P-51D-5s (44-13555) issued to the 335th FS, this P-51B was lost on 6 June 1944 with Flg Off Walter Smith at the controls, his flight of four Mustangs being bounced by 15 German fighters whilst strafing trucks near Rouen. All four American fighters were quickly shot down, killing their respective pilots – the 4th FG suffered the highest losses of any American fighter group on D-Day, with seven pilots being killed, two captured and one evading.

## 42

### P-51B-5 43-6928/*OLE-II* of Capt William 'Billy' Hovde, 358th FS/355th FG, Steeple Morden, April 1944

A member of the 355th FG from mid-1943 until August 1945, 'Billy' Hovde rose through the ranks to major, and command of the 358th FS – which he led twice. He scored a solitary kill in the P-47D, followed by three more victories in this particular P-51B and 6.5 in the P-51D (five in one mission on 5 December 1944). His final success came in April 1951, when now-Lt Col Hovde claimed a MiG-15 whilst flying an F-86A with the 4th FIW in Korea.

## 43

### P-38J-15 43-28431/*HAPPY JACK'S GO BUGGY* of Capt Jack M Ilfrey, 79th FS/20th FG, King's Cliffe, May 1944

Although a brilliant pilot, Jack Ilfrey also had a reputation for recklessness both on the ground and in the air. Despite a spell in America after the completion of his first tour in May 1943, his 'history' followed him from the MTO to the ETO when he started his second tour, in England, with the 79th FS/20th FG in April 1944. Ilfrey tried to live up to his colourful reputation as often as possible, finding his various escapades (and the subsequent punishments) the best release for the tension of daily air combat. His two aerial victories with the 79th FS came whilst flying this J-15 on 24 May 1944 during a bomber escort to Berlin. Ilfrey climbed

into the Bf 109 top cover and shot one down at 30,000 ft before inadvertently ramming a second, losing about four feet of wing and sending the German fighter down in flames. Although he survived this mission, Ilfrey went down in this same fighter on 13 June 1944 when it was hit by fire during a strafing mission on Angers airfield, in France. He managed to evade capture and returned to King's Cliffe, where he subsequently served as the 79th FS's Operations Officer and then CO from 27 September to 9 December 1944.

## 44

### P-47D-22 42-26044/*Silver Lady* of Maj Leslie Smith, 61st FS/56th FG, Boxted, May 1944

Although seven-kill ace Les Smith was assigned to fly this aircraft (one of the few unpainted P-47s in the 56th FG), it proved to be a successful talisman for such aces as 'Mike' Gladych and 'Gabby' Gabreski as well.

## 45

### P-38J (serial unknown) *Janet* of Capt Thomas A White, 338th FS/55th FG, Wormingford, May 1944

White placed the six swastikas on the nose of this 338th FS P-38J even though he had scored all six of his victories with the 97th FS/82nd FG in North Africa between January and March 1943. The aircraft was named after the daughter of the squadron's Intelligence Officer, Wally Ryerson, with whom White maintained a correspondence. Sometime after the captain had left the 338th, the nose of the fighter was painted red (in the same shade as the spinners) through the first two letters of the name. No photos have been found of the P-38 wearing invasion stripes, so it seems likely that the aircraft had been taken out of service before 6 June 1944.

## 46

### P-51B-15 42-106924/*Salem Representative* of 2Lt Ralph 'Kid' Hofer, 334th FS/4th FG, Debden, May 1944

A rebellious maverick who habitually flew in a blue and orange college football shirt, the 'Kid' began his flying career in the RCAF, transferring to the AAF in June 1943. The *Salem Representative* was Hofer's third P-51B, being assigned to him in April 1944 – his first two aircraft had been lost while being flown by other pilots. This fighter had drab upper surfaces, with a very high demarcation line on the fuselage, and a red band across the fin in the same position as the discontinued recognition marking. Black recognition stripes were retained under the wings and the tailplane. An ace even before his promotion from flight officer to second lieutenant in late April, Hofer was killed in action over Yugoslavia on 2 July 1944 when he was shot down by a Bf 109. His score stood at 15 aircraft destroyed (at least four of which were downed in this aircraft) in the air and a further 15 destroyed on the ground at the time of his death.

## 47

### P-51B-10 42-106449/*Princess ELIZABETH* of 1Lt William 'Bill' Whisner, 487th FS/352nd FG, Bodney, May 1944

A veteran of the 352nd FG's P-47 operations, 'Bill' Whisner transitioned to the P-51B in the spring of 1944, bringing his solitary Thunderbolt kill with him. His first Mustang was 42-106449, and he claimed just a half-share with it on 30 May. The name *Princess ELIZABETH* was chosen for the aircraft not by its pilot or crew chief, but rather a senior AAF Press Corps officer who wanted to impress the future Queen of England during her visit to Bodney. Whisner was unaware of this until after the artwork had been applied, and he was not best pleased (either with the nickname or the attendant press publicity). Indeed, his next Mustang (P-51D-10 44-14237) was nicknamed *Moonbeam McSWINE!* *Princess Elizabeth* was yet another Mustang lost on D-Day, the fighter being one of two 487th FS P-51Bs downed by flak in the early evening whilst attacking assorted ground targets. Its pilot, Lt Robert Butler, bailed out over recently-won Allied territory, and he returned to Bodney within 24 hours. Ending the war with 15.5 aerial and 3 ground kills, Whisner enjoyed further success during the Korean War, claiming 5.5 MiG-15s destroyed whilst flying F-86Es with the 4th and 51st FIWs.

## 48

### P-51B-10 42-106448/ *THE HUN HUNTER FROM TEXAS* of 1Lt Henry 'Baby' Brown, 354th FS/355th FG, Steeple Morden, May 1944

Although Henry Brown scored a number of his kills in other Mustangs, this P-51B was the original aircraft assigned to him when North American fighters were issued to the 354th FS in early 1944. As his kill tally grew (he scored three victories in 42-106448), the red stripe that had been originally applied as a backdrop for his successes had to be expanded into a full panel! By the time he was shot down by flak and captured in October 1944, Brown's tally had risen to 14.2 aerial and 14.5 ground kills – this made him the 355th FG's ranking ace.

## 49

### P-51B-15 43-24769/ *MISSOURI MAULER* of Capt Willard 'Millie' Millikan, 336th FS/4th FG, Debden, May 1944

After having a stipulated $350 worth of dental work carried out, 'Millie' Millikan was allowed to join the Army Air Corps only to be 'washed out' of flying training for an 'inherent lack of flying ability'. Even in the RCAF, which he subsequently joined, the future ace showed little promise, and he was advised to become a ferry pilot. Despite a reputation for emphasising protection of the bombers, and supporting other members of his flight (rather than chasing after enemy fighters 'hell-for-leather'), Millikan quickly became an ace, eventually amassing 13 victories. Ten of these were scored in the P-51B, although only his final kill (a Bf 109, claimed on 22 May 1944 near Kiel) was achieved in this particular aircraft. Millikan's war ended on 30 May 1944 when his wingman collided with 43-24769 whilst trying to avoid flak. Both pilots bailed out and became PoWs, although Millikan later escaped in the final weeks of the war in Europe. The ace later saw action during the Korean conflict, leading a squadron of F-84 Thunderjets.

## 50

### P-38J-10 42-68008/ *Touché* of Lt Col James Herren, CO of the 434th FS/479th FG, Wattisham, June 1944

A popular commander, Herren led the 434th FS during its first months with the Eighth Air Force from May through to September 1944. This unit provided three of the 479th FG's four aces, all of whom had been led with deftness and determination by Herren during their first crucial combat sorties. He scored all his P-38 aerial victories on

26 September 1944 when the 479th garnered 29 confirmed claims for just a single loss. Herren also claimed a Ju 52/3m on the ground and shared a stationary He 111 with another pilot when the group destroyed a number of aircraft during a series of strafing runs on 18 August 1944. He was finally killed in action in a P-51D during yet another ground attack mission in October 1944. P-38J-10 *Touché* was unusual in sporting a black ID disc on its twin tails, for the 434th FS had previously used a white triangle on its OD Lightnings whilst the 435th used the circle marking – perhaps this aircraft had been 'acquired' from the latter unit at some point. The squadron painter reputedly hated the tedium of accurately masking off the tail symbols, and he was quite pleased when the 434th adopted the simple all-red rudder marking in August 1944.

## 51

### P-51B-15 43-24824/ *OLD CROW* of Capt Clarence 'Bud' Anderson, 362nd FS/357th FG, Leiston, June 1944

A member of the highly successful 357th FG, Californian 'Bud' Anderson was one of a number of pilots who favoured the P-51B over the 'improved' P-51D. The latter version was made available to him at Leiston from late May 1944 onwards, but the group's third ranking ace (16.25 aerial victories and one ground kill) stuck with the B-model through to the end of his first tour. 'The Ds had begun arriving in the spring of 1944, and I got my own when I came back from leave. I could have had one of the first ones in May, but my earlier B-model was working so well, and I was so close to the end of my tour, that rather then take some new airplane and shake all the bugs out, I decided to stay with the *OLD CROW* I had', Anderson explained in his autobiography, *To Fly and Fight*. The inspiration behind the fighter's unique nickname was also revealed in the same volume; 'I tell my non-drinking friends that all my fighters were named after the smartest bird that flies in the sky, the crow, but my drinking buddies all know they were named after that good old Kentucky straight bourbon whiskey!' This particular aircraft was flown by Anderson from late February until he returned to the USA on leave in July. It was then passed on to fellow 362nd FS flightmate Bill Overstreet, who renamed the fighter *BERLIN EXPRESS* and continued to fly it through to the end of his tour some months later.

## 52

### P-51B-5 43-6933/ *SPEEDBALL ALICE* of 1Lt Donald Bochkay, 363rd FS/357th FG, Leiston, June 1944

The 357th initially flew its Mustangs without distinctive unit insignia, apart from two-letter unit codes and individual aircraft letters. The standard VIII Fighter Command white nose band and spinner was soon replaced by red and yellow chequers, and the group retained this marking through to VE-Day. Initially serving in the army as a private within the 7th Infantry Division, Bochkay transferred to the Army Air Corps in 1942 and joined the 357th FG in May 1943. During his two combat tours in the ETO with the 363rd FS, he frequently flew as part of a flight of four aircraft that comprised Jim Browning (a seven-victory ace who was killed in action on 9 February 1945), the legendary 'Chuck' Yeager (11.5 aerial kills) and 'Bud' Anderson. Bochkay finished the war as the 363rd FS's CO, having scored 13.833 aerial victories.

# FIGURE PLATES

## 1

Lt Col Dave Schilling, Deputy CO of the 56th FG at Hales-worth in March 1944, is seen wearing olive drab (OD) shirt and pants, topped off with an officer's overseas cap – note the black and gold officer braid on the cap. He has a silk scarf around his neck  – synonymous with fighter pilots the world over, scarves were worn to reduce neck chafing whilst pilots constantly 'swivelled' their heads to look out of the cockpit in search of the enemy. Schilling wears Russet brown low-quarter shoes on his feet, whilst his Mae West is RAF 1941 pattern, with distinctive securing tie-tapes. Finally, the zip-closed pouch attached the right harness strap of his B-8 parachute (with AN-6510 seat pack) contains first-aid dressings.

## 2

Col 'Hub' Zemke, CO of the 56th FG at Halesworth in December 1943, wears a M-1926 officer's issue short wool overcoat over his dark OD shirt and pants. His shoes are again Russet brown low-quarter style, whilst his gloves are B-10 Russet leather. On his head, Zemke wears his prized service hat with all important soft crown ('50 mission crush' style), created by the removal of the interior stiffeners – typical AAF practice, done so as to enable a headset to be worn over the hat.

## 3

Lt Robert Johnson of the 61st FS/56th FG at Halesworth in October 1943 has an RAF 'C' type flying helmet on his head, fitted with standard US R-14 receivers. The latter were not a perfect fit in the rubber mounts of the British helmets, which meant that they were invariably taped into place, as can be seen here. B-7 goggles complete his headwear. Johnson's Mae West is a B-3 type, worn over a favourite A-2 leather jacket. His trousers are OD 'mustard' shade, whilst his shoes are GI service issue. Finally, Johnson's gloves are the officer-issue chamois-leather type.

## 4

Maj Gerry Johnson of the 360th FS/356th FG at Martlesham Heath in January 1944. Like his namesake in the previous artwork, he is wearing an RAF 'C' type helmet with B-7 goggles. Note the British style 'bell-shaped' jack plug in his hand, which the Americans had adapted to allow the helmet's receivers to work with their own system. The attached oxygen mask is a Type A-14. His remaining attire is identical to Bob Johnson's with the exception of his Russet brown low-quarter shoes

## 5

Capt 'Gabby' Gabreski, CO of the 61st FS/56th FG at Hor-sham St Faith in June 1943, is wearing light olive drab (shade 54) shirt, pants and 'overseas' cap, which was a combination widely chosen by ETO pilots as their woollen material made them warmer in a cold cockpit than cotton khakis. Over his A-2 jacket he has on an RAF 1941 pattern Mae West, whilst his flying boots are 1936 pattern from the same source.

## 6

Lt Col Eugene Roberts, Deputy CO of the 78th FG at Duxford in October 1943, has on officer's dark olive drab (shade 51) shirt and overseas cap, whilst his trousers are shade 54 'pinks'. Note the khaki tie tucked into his shirt as per regulations, and the silver pilot's wings pinned to his shirt above the left breast pocket. These are three inches in size, although there was a smaller two-inch size made specifically for wearing on shirts. On Roberts' left collar point is the gold/silver winged-prop device of the AAF, whilst his insignia of rank – a silver oak leaf – is pinned to the front left side of his garrison ('overseas') cap. Finally, his shoes are commercial pattern, rather than regulation Oxford-style lace-ups.

## 7

Lt James Morris of the 77th FS/20th FG at King's Cliffe in February 1944. He is wearing a US Army tank crewman's winter jacket and bib overalls, over which a regulation issue B-3 life preserver has been donned. His gloves are fur-lined gauntlet style A-9s, his helmet/goggles combination identical to Lindol Graham's (see commentary below), and his mask an A-10. Finally, the ace's uniform is completed by a pair of heavy A-2A double-strap flying boots and a white neck scarf.

## 8

Capt Lindol 'Lindy' Graham of the 79th FS/20th FG at King's Cliffe in September 1943. The future ace is wearing woollen OD trousers (turned up rather than tucked into his Russet GI issue boots) and a B-10 jacket, minus its fur collars. Beneath his khaki jacket, Graham has on an officers' issue khaki shirt and matching tie, the former complete with rank tabs. His helmet is ex-RAF issue, being an early-war Type C – the attached goggles are USAAF-issue B-7s, as are the pilot's B-2 gloves. Finally, his parachute pack is a B-8.

# INDEX

References to illustrations are shown in **bold**. Plates are prefixed 'pl.' or 'fig.pl' with page numbers in brackets, e.g. pl.**45**(92, 141).